Contents

Acknowledgments ....
Introduction 1
How to Use This Guide 9
Trail Finder 11
Map Legend 13

The Hikes

1. Riverwalk: Tonawanda Parks 14
2. Wilson-Tuscarora State Park 18
3. Erie Canalway Trail: Lockport to Gasport 22
4. Royalton Ravine County Park 26
5. Buckhorn Island State Park: Long Trail 30
6. Niagara Falls State Park: Great Gorge
   Railway Trail 34
7. Devil's Hole State Park 38
8. Ellicott Creek Trailway 42
9. Walton Woods 47
10. Akron Falls Park: Conservation Trail 51
11. Iroquois National Wildlife Refuge:
    Swallow Hollow Trail 55
12. Reinstein Woods Nature Preserve: History, Beech
    Tree, Footprint, and Lily Pond Trails Loop 59
13. Tillman Road Wildlife Management Area 64
14. Hunter's Creek County Park 69
15. Emery Park 73
16. Chestnut Ridge Park: Eternal Flame Trail 77
17. Erie County Forest 81
18. Deer Lick Conservation Area 86
19. Beaver Meadow Audubon Center 91

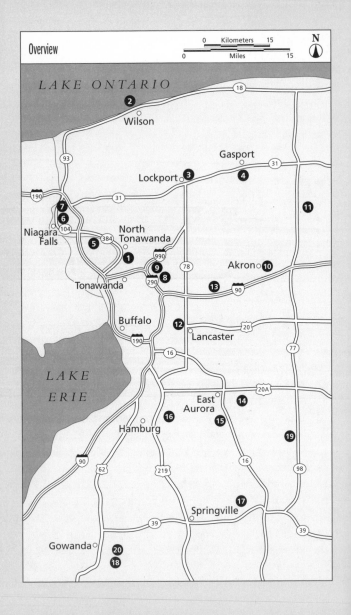

Overview

0 — Kilometers — 15
0 — Miles — 15

N

LAKE ONTARIO

② Wilson

⑱

Gasport

Lockport ③ ④

93

190

31

⑦
⑥
104

Niagara
Falls

⑤ 384

North
Tonawanda

①

990

⑨
⑧

78

290

11

Akron ⑩

⑬ 90

Tonawanda

Buffalo

190

⑫ Lancaster

16

20

77

LAKE
ERIE

East
Aurora ⑭

⑯ ⑮

20A

Hamburg

⑲

90

62

219

16

98

Springville ⑰

39

39

Gowanda ⑳
⑱

20. Zoar Valley Multiple Use Area:
    Valentine Flats Trail... 96

Clubs and Trail Groups... 101
About the Author 103

Acknowledgments

First, I must thank Scott Adams, executive editor at Falcon-Guides, for determining in late November that he needed a manuscript for a Buffalo hiking guide by mid-April. I admit to initial consternation, but in the end I would not trade away the opportunity to appreciate western New York's legendary winter and roaring spring from the outside. The new skills I developed, including taking notes with gloves on and climbing down icy hills, will only enrich my experiences next winter. I extend many thanks to Scott and to everyone at FalconGuides, whose work brings so many of our books to fruition.

To my brilliant agent, Regina Ryan, I am undyingly grateful for all that she does to manage the business of publishing on my behalf.

The western New York members of Geneseebirds, the discussion list for Rochester- and Buffalo-area birders, were generous with trail suggestions and contacts. My thanks to Carl Mrozek, Ann Beebe, Chuck Rosenberg, Gerry Rising, Jeffrey Reed, Willie D'Anna, and Jerry Lazarczyk for pointing me in directions I may not have gone on my own.

Several managers of beautiful natural spaces extended their assistance as well. Meaghan Boice-Green of Reinstein Woods was especially helpful. I appreciate the help I received from David Clark at Buckhorn Island, Lee Ann Cogar at Niagara County, Angela Berti and Barry Virgilio of New York State Parks, Jared Jackson at Erie County, Patrick McGlew from The Nature Conservancy, Erin Agins at the New York State Canal Corporation, and John Curtiss at the New York State Department of Environmental Conservation.

I have so many friends to whom I am grateful, but Martha Schermerhorn, Martin Winer, Ken Horowitz, and Rose-Anne Moore stand out from this group for their unflagging encouragement and support. In particular, Martin paced many of these trails with us without a word of complaint about soggy paths, ankle-deep mud, or daunting hills. I can't say as much about myself.

And finally, to my husband, Nic, who was at my side on nearly every trail, keeping me from getting hopelessly lost and carrying supplies I repeatedly forgot—I am, as always, impossibly thankful and totally smitten.

Introduction

In my years as a student at the University at Buffalo, living in Peter Porter Quad in the venerable Ellicott Complex, I often did my best to escape on a sunny, usually windy Sunday afternoon and trudge around campus and beyond. Major development had not yet arrived in Amherst and Williamsville in the 1970s, so wide swaths of woods surrounded the campus and extended for what seemed like miles. I tramped blissfully past ponds and through stands of huge trees in what I now know to be Walton Woods, and wandered the route that would become the Ellicott Creek Trailway. I came to know the natural lands near campus as my solace, my break from the undergraduate grind of deadlines and exams.

What a natural progression, then, to come home to these lands several decades later, and to rediscover the topography around Buffalo with a new level of fascination. Had I known then about the natural wonderland at Reinstein Woods, the adventure of hiking down Royalton Ravine, the extraordinary terrain reconstruction performed by two creeks in Zoar Valley, or the hypnotic force of water against rock in the Niagara River Gorge—well, I might never have made it to a single class.

Residents rarely think of the Buffalo area as a treasury of dramatic natural phenomena, but the fact is that northwestern New York State is loaded with evidence of millions of years of geological history. North of the city, the Niagara Escarpment exerts supreme influence over the landscape, providing the cliff over which a natural wonder of the world takes form. Were it not for this ridge extending east to Rochester's Genesee Valley and west to the Wisconsin-Illinois border north of Chicago, there would be no Niagara Falls—and the exceptional Niagara Gorge, with its 200-foot-high shale walls and harder, dolomite limestone cap, would be nothing more than a conventional riverbed. This remarkable result of unequal erosion gives us some of the most exciting vistas in the northeastern United States, bringing us close to raging river rapids, whirlpools, and standing waves.

Moving south and east through Erie County, more surprises are hidden within small towns and in clusters of preserved lands. Creeks born as tiny streams eons ago continue to erode the shale around them, creating Hunter's Creek's peaceful ridgelines and the rocky ravine at Emery Park in Aurora. A trick of nature allows natural gas to escape in tiny quantities at the bottom of Chestnut Ridge Park's striking ravine, creating a fuel source for the "eternal flame" perpetuated by amazed visitors with matches and lighters. An underground spring bubbles to the surface in Deer Lick Preserve, aided by a simple pipe provided by The Nature Conservancy . . . while an overlook just a few hundred feet away provides a viewpoint for the 400-foot-deep canyon carved by the rushing Cattaraugus Creek below.

Beyond the ravines, wetlands filled with singing amphibians and migrating birds beckon to wildlife lovers of all stripes. The emergent marsh at Iroquois National Wildlife Refuge becomes home to a choral masterpiece in spring, as seven different species of frogs raise their voices in mating song. The northwestern counties play an important role in the North American flyway in spring, as tens of thousands of waterfowl touch down on ponds, lakes, and the Niagara River—particularly at Buckhorn Island—to rest and feed before proceeding across the Great Lakes. Songbirds—warblers, vireos, sparrows, thrushes, and more—gather in the shrubs and trees in Reinstein Woods Nature Preserve in Depew, Beaver Meadow Audubon Center in North Java, Wilson-Tuscarora State Park on the Lake Ontario shoreline, and Tillman Road Wildlife Management Area in Clarence, where food and lifesaving cover are plentiful. Furry creatures from tiny shrews to foxes, raccoons, and beavers find homes in the dense Erie County Forest and in many other stands of northern hardwoods and evergreens.

As in every city, some Buffalo-area residents prefer the leisure of paved pathways and groomed lawns to the packed earth, unpredictable environment, and wild critters in nature preserves. Enlightened teams at the Town of Amherst, the City of Buffalo, and Erie County have provided for these folks as well with the Ellicott Creek Trailway and River-walk, two carefully maintained fitness trails through level, developed areas close to residential neighborhoods. The Erie Canalway Trail brings another paved, long-distance pathway into the mix, combining some state history with a great walk through small towns, cultivated farmland, and pocket parks.

With so many options for day hikes, residents and visitors will find plenty of outdoor adventures that showcase the best of northwestern New York—and all less than an hour's drive from the city of Buffalo.

Weather

When the annual miracle of spring arrives in Buffalo and the city and county burst into bloom, there's no beating this area for the beauty and euphoria the warmer season brings.

The sun shines up to 67 percent of the time from May through August, and idyllic spring and summer days can average in the 70s and 80s, with occasional spikes into the 90s in June or July and cooler temperatures at night. Heavy rains often arrive in June, August, and September, although they rarely last for more than a day or two at a time. Buffalo has no dry season, so be prepared for rain anytime you visit.

To truly appreciate this transformation to the Technicolor spring and summer seasons in northwestern New York, however, we must face the Buffalo area's impressive winters.

Winter temperatures average in the low 30s, with significant dips into the 20s, 10s, and single digits in January, February, and March. Check the "wind chill" before making a winter hike, as the air can feel much colder than the temperature indicates. The annual February thaw can push temperatures into the 50s for a few days, but the cold will return, usually lasting into mid-April. Snow is guaranteed—an average winter sees somewhere between 100 and 150 inches, although not all at once—and much of this is "lake effect snow," which can fall even when the radar shows clear skies. In the winter months from November through January, the Buffalo area sees the sun about 28 percent of the time.

Fall equals spring in its spectacle, with days in the 50s and 60s, bright blue skies, and foliage panoramas throughout the area's parks and preserves.

Park and Preserve Regulations

Generally, you will find the lands listed in this book both accessible and fairly easy to navigate. Only one of the parks and preserves listed charges an admission fee (though some suggest a donation), so you have free access to any trail you'd like to explore.

While some of the parks have picnic areas with trash receptacles, most of the parks and preserves are "carry-in, carry-out" areas. This means that you must take all of your trash with you for disposal outside of the park. Glass containers are not permitted in any of the parks.

In all cases, dogs and other pets must be leashed—and some preserves do not permit pets. You will see dogs running free in some parks, but park regulations and county leash laws prohibit this. It's also illegal to leave your dog's droppings in the park; you can face fines for not cleaning up after your pet.

If you're a gun owner, you will need to leave your weapon at home when entering an Erie or Niagara County park, as only law enforcement officers are permitted to carry guns on these lands. Hunting is not permitted in any of the parks and preserves in this book, except for Zoar Valley Multiple Use Area and Wilson-Tuscarora State Park, although fishing (with a license) is encouraged in many of the parks.

Safety and Preparation

There is little to fear when hiking in upstate New York, whether you're stepping down into the Chestnut Ridge ravine or hiking through Erie County Forest. Some basic safety precautions and intelligent preparation will make all of your hikes calamity-free.

- **Wear proper footwear.** A good, correctly fitting pair of hiking shoes or boots can make all the difference on a daylong hike, or even on a short walk. Look for socks that wick away moisture, or add sock liners to your footwear system.

- **Carry a first-aid kit** to deal with blisters, cuts and scrapes, and insect bites and stings. Insects abound in late spring and summer in northwestern New York, especially near wetlands, ponds, lakes, and creeks, so wear insect repellent and carry after-bite ointment or cream to apply to itchy spots.

- **Carry water.** Don't try drinking from the river, creeks, ponds, or other bodies of water unless you can filter or treat the water first. Your best bet is to carry your own—at least a quart for any hike.

- **Dress in layers,** no matter what the season. If you're a vigorous hiker, you'll want to peel off a layer or two even in the dead of winter. On a summer evening, the air can cool suddenly after sunset, and rain clouds can erupt with little preamble.

- **Bring your cell phone.** All but the most remote trails in western New York have cell coverage, so if you do get into a jam, help is just a phone call away. (Set it to vibrate while you're on trail, however, as a courtesy to the rest of us.)

- **Leave wildlife alone.** Northwestern New York State once was home to the timber rattlesnake, but scientists believe this species to be extirpated from the area. Black bear sightings are very rare. As a general rule, don't approach wildlife of any kind. If you do see a bear, don't go close to it; if your presence changes its behavior, you're too close. Keep your distance and the bear will most likely do the same.

Zero Impact

Many trails in the Buffalo area are heavily used year-round.

As trail users and advocates, we must be especially vigilant to make sure our passage leaves no lasting mark. Here are some basic guidelines for preserving trails in the region:

- Pack out all your own trash, including biodegradable items like orange peels. You might also pack out garbage left by less-considerate hikers.

- Don't approach or feed any wild creatures; the gray squirrel eyeing your snack food is best able to survive if it remains self-reliant. Feeding ducks and geese can spread illnesses between the birds when they come into contact while chasing bits of bread or corn. Please don't feed them.

- Don't pick wildflowers or gather rocks, antlers, feathers, and other treasures along the trail. Removing these items will only take away from the next hiker's experience.

- Avoid damaging trailside soils and plants by remaining on the established route. This is also a good rule of thumb for avoiding poison ivy and poison sumac, common regional trailside irritants.

- Be courteous by not making loud noises while hiking.

- Many of these trails are multiuse, which means you'll share them with other hikers, trail runners, bikers, and equestrians. Familiarize yourself with the proper trail etiquette, yielding the trail when appropriate.

- Use restrooms or outhouses at trailheads or along the trail.

Land Management Agencies

These government and nonprofit organizations manage most of the public lands described in this guide. They can provide further information on these hikes and other trails in the greater Buffalo area.

Buffalo Audubon Society, 1610 Welch Rd., North Java, NY 14113; (585) 457-3228; www.buffaloaudubon.com

Erie County Parks and Recreation, 95 Franklin St., Room 1359, Buffalo, NY 14202; (716) 858-8355; www.erie.gov/parks

The Nature Conservancy, Central & Western New York Chapter, 1048 University Ave., Rochester, NY 14607; (716) 699-8386; www.nature.org

New York State Canal System, 200 Southern Blvd., Albany, NY 12201; 800-4CANAL4 (422-6254); www.nyscanals.gov

New York State Department of Environmental Conservation, 270 Michigan Ave., Buffalo, NY 14203; (716) 851-7010; www.dec.ny.gov/outdoor/

Niagara County Parks & Recreation, 59 Park Ave., Suite 205, Lockport, NY 14094; (716) 439-7950; www.niagaracounty.com/Parks/

Niagara Falls State Park, P.O. Box 773, Niagara Falls, Grand Island, NY 14302; (716) 278-0337; www.niagarafallsstatepark.com

Town of Amherst, 5583 Main St., Williamsville, NY 14221; (716) 631-7013; www.amherst.ny.us

How to Use This Guide

This guide is designed to be simple and easy to use. Each hike is described with a map and summary information that delivers the trail's vital statistics, including length, difficulty, fees and permits, park hours, canine compatibility, and trail contacts. Directions to the trailhead are also provided, along with a general description of what you'll see along the way. A detailed route finder (Miles and Directions) sets forth mileages between significant landmarks along the trail.

Hike Selection

This guide describes trails that are accessible to every hiker, whether visiting from out of town or living in the greater Buffalo area. The hikes are no longer than 8 miles round-trip, and some are considerably shorter. They range in difficulty from flat excursions perfect for a family outing to more challenging treks along the area's gorges and ravines. While these trails are among the best, keep in mind that nearby trails, often in the same park or preserve, may offer options better suited to your needs. I've sought to space hikes throughout the Erie, Niagara, Wyoming, and Genesee County areas, so wherever your starting point, you'll find a great easy day hike nearby.

Difficulty Ratings

These are all easy hikes, but easy is a relative term. Some would argue that no hike involving any kind of climbing is easy, but in the Buffalo area, hills and ravines are a fact of life. To aid in the selection of a hike that suits particular needs and abilities, each is rated easy, moderate, or more challenging. Bear in mind that even the most challenging routes can be made easy by hiking within your limits and taking rests when you need them.

- **Easy** hikes are generally short and flat, taking no longer than an hour to complete.
- **Moderate** hikes involve increased distance and relatively mild changes in elevation, and will take one to two hours to complete.
- **More challenging** hikes feature some steep stretches, greater distances, and generally take longer than two hours to complete.

These are completely subjective ratings—consider that what you think is easy is entirely dependent on your level of fitness and the adequacy of your gear (primarily shoes). If you are hiking with a group, you should select a hike with a rating that's appropriate for the least fit and prepared in your party.

Approximate hiking times are based on the assumption that on flat ground, most walkers average two miles per hour. Adjust that rate by the steepness of the terrain and your level of fitness (subtract time if you're an aerobic animal and add time if you're hiking with kids), and you have a ballpark hiking duration. Be sure to add more time if you plan to picnic or take part in other activities, like birdwatching or photography.

Trail Finder

Best Hikes for Birders

5   Buckhorn Island State Park: Long Trail (page 30)

11   Iroquois National Wildlife Refuge: Swallow Hollow Trail (page 55)

12   Reinstein Woods Nature Preserve: History, Beech Tree, Footprint, and Lily Pond Trails Loop (page 59)

13   Tillman Road Wildlife Management Area (page 64)

17   Erie County Forest (page 81)

19   Beaver Meadow Audubon Center (page 91)

Best Hikes for Waterfalls

4   Royalton Ravine County Park (page 26)

6   Niagara Falls State Park: Great Gorge Railway Trail (page 34)

10   Akron Falls Park: Conservation Trail (page 51)

14   Hunter's Creek County Park (page 69)

15   Emery Park (page 73)

16   Chestnut Ridge Park: Eternal Flame Trail (page 77)

18   Deer Lick Conservation Area (page 86)

Best Hikes for Panoramic Views

1   Riverwalk: Tonawanda Parks (page 14)

7   Devil's Hole State Park (page 38)

20   Zoar Valley Multiple Use Area: Valentine Flats Trial (page 96)

Best Hikes for Fall Foliage

2   Wilson–Tuscarora State Park (page 18)
10   Akron Falls Park: Conservation Trail (page 51)
14   Hunter's Creek County Park (page 69)
17   Erie County Forest (page 81)
18   Deer Lick Conservation Area (page 86)
19   Beaver Meadow Audubon Center (page 91)
20   Zoar Valley Multiple Use Area: Valentine Flats Trail (page 96)

Best Hikes for Fitness Walkers

1   Riverwalk: Tonawanda Parks (page 14)
3   Erie Canalway Trail: Lockport to Gasport (page 22)
8   Ellicott Creek Trailway (page 42)
9   Walton Woods (page 47)

Map Legend

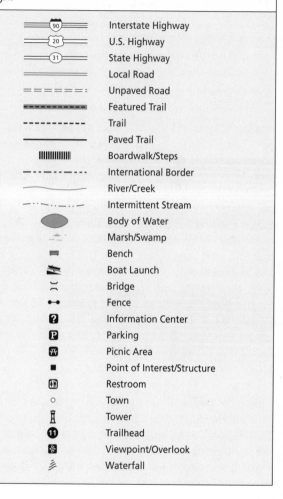

	Interstate Highway
	U.S. Highway
	State Highway
	Local Road
	Unpaved Road
	Featured Trail
	Trail
	Paved Trail
	Boardwalk/Steps
	International Border
	River/Creek
	Intermittent Stream
	Body of Water
	Marsh/Swamp
	Bench
	Boat Launch
	Bridge
	Fence
	Information Center
	Parking
	Picnic Area
	Point of Interest/Structure
	Restroom
	Town
	Tower
	Trailhead
	Viewpoint/Overlook
	Waterfall

1 Riverwalk: Tonawanda Parks

This world-class fitness pathway follows the course of the Niagara River from the city of Buffalo to Niagara Falls. This Tonawanda section provides leisurely walking through two developed parks.

Distance: 5.2 miles out-and-back

Approximate hiking time: 2.5 hours

Difficulty: Easy

Trail surface: Paved, with lines separating walkers and bicyclists

Best season: Apr through Nov

Other trail users: Joggers, bicyclists, inline skaters

Canine compatibility: Dogs permitted on leash with restrictions in Niawanda Park: May–Sept, dogs are allowed only 6–9 a.m. Leashed dogs permitted anytime in Isle View Park.

Fees and permits: None

Schedule: Open daily dawn to dusk

Maps: Erie County Parks and Recreation, www.erie.gov/parks/riverwalk_map.asp

Trailhead facilities: Restrooms in three places along this section of trail; vendors in Isle View County Park

Trail contact: Erie County Parks and Recreation, 95 Franklin St., Room 1359, Buffalo, NY 14202; (716) 858-8355; www.erie.gov/parks

Finding the trailhead: From Buffalo, take I-190 north to exit 17 (NY 266 / River Road). Turn right at Niagara Street and follow NY 266 to Niagara Shore Drive, on your left. Turn left on Niagara Shore Drive and continue left along the road to the parking lot on your right (behind Tonawanda City Hall at 200 Niagara Street). Park here and begin the trail going south, with the river on your right. GPS: N43 01.167' / W78 53.250'

The Hike

This carefully planned and well-maintained recreational trail offers the kind of outdoor experience that attracts families with young children, long-distance cyclists, energetic inline skaters, and seniors maintaining their fitness—so you can expect to see plenty of people as you walk this section of the Riverwalk. The total trail extends into downtown Buffalo to the south and connects with the Barge Canal towpath trail here in Tonawanda, continuing all the way to Niagara Falls and on into Canada. On this trail segment, you'll cross Niawanda Park and Isle View County Park, two developed areas with green lawns, gazebos, benches, and picnic tables—and quick access to snacks and ice cream on the parallel Niagara Street.

A white line divides the paved path, with the pedestrian lane designated to the right. All of the amenities of a modern fitness trail are available: Signposts every half-mile provide location numbers (you are at post #9) and emergency phone numbers, while restrooms appear at regular intervals.

What makes this trail special is the Niagara River, a grand sight that can dazzle walkers on a sunny day. The connecting waterway from Lake Erie to Lake Ontario, this river flows relatively calmly through the Tonawanda area, giving no hint of the turbulence to come as it reaches the Niagara Escarpment and tumbles over the edge as Niagara Falls. Grand Island provides the "Isle View" across the water: The largest island in the river actually splits the river flow in two, with the two parts coming together again at Buckhorn Island State Park at the island's northwest end. More than 18,000 people make this island their home.

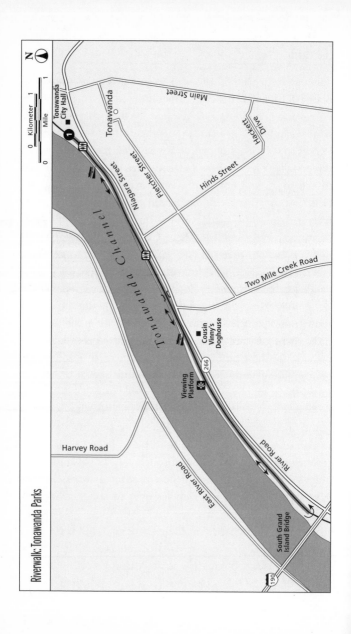

You'll see many lucky residents' waterfront residences as you traverse the Riverwalk.

Miles and Directions

0.0 Begin the trail at the parking lot behind Tonawanda City Hall. Walk left, with the river on your right.

0.2 There are restrooms here.

0.3 A boat launch provides easy water access for trailers bringing motorboats.

0.8 Here is another building with restrooms.

1.2 There's a bridge over an inlet here. This is a good spot to look for winter waterfowl on the river, even as late as mid-Apr. In about 300 feet, Isle View Park begins—you'll see Cousin Vinny's Doghouse snack bar (open in summer), a gazebo, and a river-viewing platform with picnic tables and benches.

1.4 Another boat launch provides river access.

1.5 There's another viewing platform here, with benches and picnic tables.

2.6 You've walked the length of Isle View Park to the South Grand Island Bridge. From here, the path continues into downtown Buffalo. If you're ready, turn around and retrace your steps to the parking lot where your walk began.

5.2 You're back at the parking lot behind City Hall.

2 Wilson-Tuscarora State Park

On the Lake Ontario shoreline, this pleasant walk leads through the Twelve Mile Creek watershed to an old-growth woods and a thriving wetland.

Distance: 1.4-mile loop

Approximate hiking time: 1 hour

Difficulty: Easy

Trail surface: Mowed grass and dirt path

Best season: Apr through Nov

Other trail users: Cross-country skiers and snowshoers in winter

Canine compatibility: Leashed dogs permitted

Fees and permits: Admission fee in season

Schedule: Open daily dawn to dusk

Maps: New York State Parks, http://nysparks.state.ny.us/ gmaps/

Trailhead facilities: The bathhouse/lifeguard station has restrooms and water in season. No water or restrooms in winter.

Trail contact: Wilson Tuscarora State Park, 3371 Lake Rd., Wilson, NY 14072; (716) 751-6361; http://nysparks.state.ny.us/parks/info.asp?parkID=31

Special considerations: Small game and waterfowl hunting is permitted in season; wear a bright color (orange is best). Parks roads are plowed in winter for limited use only.

Finding the trailhead: From Buffalo, take I-190 north to exit 25B (NY 104 / Robert Moses Parkway). Merge onto Upper Mountain Road, and then onto NY 104 east toward Lewiston. Take the ramp onto NY 18 east and turn right on NY 18 (Lake Road). Continue 10.2 miles to the park. Drive along the park road past the pavilions and bathhouse to the last gravel parking lot. The trailhead is in the southeast corner of this lot. GPS: N43 18.709' / W78 50.644'

The Hike

A favorite with cross-country skiers as well as day-hikers, this park's 476 acres of mature woods, wetlands, and meadows provide a peek into the wildlife-rich wilderness along relatively flat, easy trails. While the longer trail in this park crosses open meadow and follows along the highway, our recommended trail takes hikers into woods and wetlands to explore the edge of the marsh and the East Branch of Twelve Mile Creek.

Mourning cloak and cabbage white butterflies float in front of you in spring and summer as you begin the trail. Watch for yellow warblers and common yellowthroats as you follow the edge of the creek into the wooded areas, and listen for the Carolina wren's "teakettle, teakettle, teakettle" call, as well as the swamp sparrow's rapid, one-tone trill. Ring-necked pheasants are resident here; one may dash across the trail or flush from the tall grasses.

The wetland areas offer excellent viewing for great blue and green herons, and even the occasional Virginia rail or sora. Watch for beavers as you walk along the marsh, and listen for woodpeckers in the old-growth woods.

One way to recognize the oldest trees is by their imposing girth: A circumference greater than 36 inches qualifies as "old growth" (although some old growth trees are not this large). If you haven't brought your tape measure, look for tall trees with weirdly splayed roots, particularly impressive height, and contorted limbs; these are most likely some of the oldest trees in the woods.

If you'd like to extend your hike after you've explored this trail, turn left on the green trail at the 1.2-mile point instead of taking the blue trail back to the parking lot. The green route will add about 2 miles to your walk.

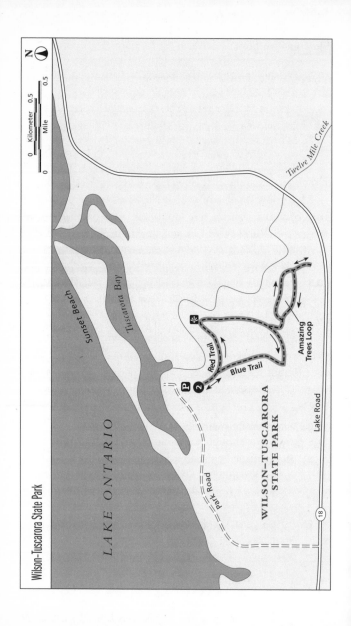

Wilson-Tuscarora State Park

LAKE ONTARIO

Sunset Beach

Tuscarora Bay

Twelve Mile Creek

Park Road

Red Trail

Blue Trail

Amazing
Trees Loop

WILSON–TUSCARORA
STATE PARK

Lake Road

18

N

0   Kilometer   0.5

0   Mile   0.5

Miles and Directions

0.0 Begin the trail at the parking lot. Follow the red trail, which goes straight ahead. (The blue trail goes to the right.)

0.2 Continue on the red trail, to the right around the loop. In a few steps you'll come to a short trail to the left that leads to an overlook, with a terrific view of Twelve Mile Creek. When you're ready, continue on the red trail, uphill to the left as you come back from the overlook. Watch for beavers as you follow along the edge of the wetland. Woodpeckers are easy to spot in the trees here at any time of year.

0.4 The red and blue trails meet here; turn left and continue on the red trail. In a few feet, you'll see the blue trail cross the red again. Continue straight on the red trail, going downhill and into the woods.

0.5 The red trail loops here. Bear left and go around the loop to an interpretive sign, with information about the old-growth trees in this area. Descend gently to the wetland trail (this section can be muddy in spring). At the end of the loop, turn left.

0.7 The red trail comes out of the park here at NY 18. Retrace your steps to the last intersection, and continue around the loop (straight—don't turn right). When you get to the end of the loop, turn left.

1.0 Turn left on the blue trail.

1.1 The trails converge and make a triangle here. Turn right on the green trail. Pass along a grassy, mowed path through a young wood, between thick concentrations of leafy shrubs that line the trail. (Turning left on the green trail will take you across the park's open meadow along NY 18.)

1.2 The green and blue trails meet here. Continue straight on the green trail.

1.3 Green and blue meet here once again. Go straight on the blue trail to return to the parking lot.

1.4 Here is the parking lot.

3 Erie Canalway Trail: Lockport to Gasport

History meets recreation along this 6-mile section of the 400-mile Erie Canal towpath, an easy walk from the original canal's flight of five locks through open farmland and pocket parks.

Distance: 6-mile shuttle
Approximate hiking time: 2.5 hours
Difficulty: Moderate (for length)
Trail surface: Crushed stone with paved sections
Best season: Apr through Nov
Other trail users: Cross-country skiers, joggers, cyclists
Canine compatibility: Leashed dogs permitted
Fees and permits: None
Schedule: Open daily dawn to dusk

Maps: Erie Canalway National Heritage Corridor, www.eriecanal way.org/explore_things-to-know_ brochures-maps.htm, or order maps at www.ptny.org
Trailhead facilities: New York State Erie Canalway Museum, 80 Canal St., Lockport; merchants in Gasport
Trail contact: New York State Canal Corporation, 200 Southern Blvd., Albany, NY 12201; 800-4CANAL4 (422-6254); www .nyscanals.gov

Finding the trailhead: From Buffalo, take I-190 north to exit 24 (NY 31). Turn east on NY 31 and continue about 17 miles to Lockport. In Lockport, turn left on Spring Street and continue as Spring becomes Exchange Street. Turn left at Market Street and park in Scalzo Park (at the Lockport Locks and Erie Canalway Cruises and Heritage Center). Walk back to Exchange Street, turn left, and cross the bridge over the canal. Immediately turn right on the path to begin the hike. GPS: N43 10.623' / W78 41.150'

To park a second car in Gasport, continue on NY 31 to Main Street (also called Gasport Road) in Gasport. Turn left and cross Telegraph Road (also known as State Street). Continue across the canal on Main Street, and turn left immediately after the bridge into a gravel parking area. GPS: N43 11.994' / W78 34.576'

The Hike

Back in the early 1820s, crews of men with shovels and pickaxes began construction of the Erie Canal, the waterway that would connect the Hudson River in eastern New York State to Lake Erie, opening a trade route to the West. Engineers in charge of the project faced a daunting challenge: how to deal with the Niagara Escarpment, an obstructive ridge capped by dolomite limestone. Too hard and thick to dig through with early-nineteenth-century equipment, the escarpment would have to be surmounted with some remarkable ingenuity, the likes of which had not been seen in young America.

Today, you can still see the result: The original "Flight of Five" lock system is preserved here in downtown Lockport. Built in 1825, this five-step lock is one of the most impressive structures along the entire Erie Canal, so make a stop downtown to see it before proceeding east on the trail.

Your walk along the canal from Lockport to Gasport begins by crossing well-populated suburbs with occasional parking areas and interpretive materials. These signs of civilization drop away in a mile or so, and the trail traverses farmlands rich with this year's crops, broken by stretches of woods. Each bridge over the canal tells its own story of original construction and modernization.

Additional parking areas are indicated in the Miles and Directions below, giving you the option of choosing a

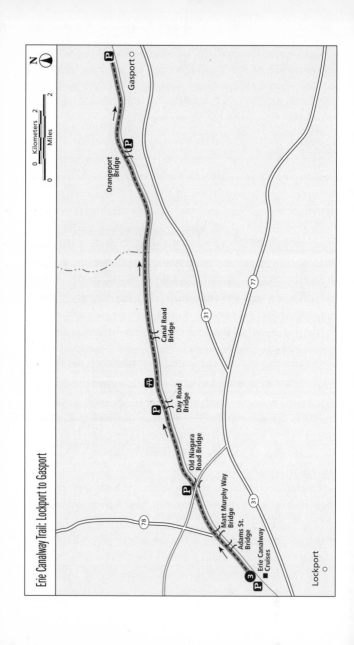

Erie Canalway Trail: Lockport to Gasport

N

0 Kilometers 2
0 Miles 2

Gasport ○

Orangeport
Bridge

Canal Road
Bridge

Day Road
Bridge

Old Niagara
Road Bridge

Matt Murphy Way
Bridge

Adams St.
Bridge

Erie Canalway
Cruises

77

31

31

78

Lockport ○

shorter hike between Lockport and Gasport. The full length offers a tranquil walk along a flat, well-maintained, and well-used trail, but there are no services along the 6-mile route, so you may wish to leave a second vehicle a little closer to your starting point.

Miles and Directions

0.0 Walk east on the flat, gravel trail.

0.1 The Adams Street Bridge crosses overhead.

0.5 The Matt Murphy Way Bridge crosses overhead.

1.1 Pass under the unmarked bridge overhead (this is Old Niagara Road in Lockport). There's a parking lot here with interpretive material about the Erie Canal path, and a map of the trail from Lockport to Rochester.

2.0 The Day Road Bridge passes overhead. This is a reconstruction of the original 1909 bridge on what was Walkman's Highway. At this point, the canal road that has paralleled the path has diverged away from the trail, and parkland fills the area to your left. Just past the bridge, there's a parking area with picnic tables.

3.0 Pass under the Canal Road Bridge. Originally built in 1910, this bridge was replaced in 1993 by the modern structure you see here.

3.7 A small, uninterpreted sign here says "118," drawing attention to an interesting water feature. The natural stream you see here goes under the canal—another remarkable feat of engineering accomplished by the canal builders.

4.9 The unmarked bridge that passes over the canal here is Orangeport Road in Orangeport, the last town before Gasport. There's a parking area here as well.

6.0 You've arrived at Gasport, at the parking area at which you left your second vehicle.

4 **Royalton Ravine County Park**

Hike to the bottom of a hidden ravine, cross a swaying cable extension bridge over a rushing stream, and ascend to the top of a four-season waterfall on this lushly wooded, secluded trail.

Distance: 2.5-mile loop or 3 miles out-and-back
Approximate hiking time: 1.25 hours
Difficulty: Moderate
Trail surface: Dirt path
Best season: Apr through Nov
Other trail users: None
Canine compatibility: Leashed dogs permitted
Fees and permits: None
Schedule: 7 a.m. to 9 p.m. daily

Maps: *National Geographic Topo! New York State* edition
Trailhead facilities: Restrooms with potable water at picnic area, open Memorial Day through Sept 30 only. No facilities Oct–May.
Trail contact: Niagara County Parks & Recreation, 59 Park Ave., Lockport, NY 14094; (716) 439-7950; www.niagaracounty .com/Parks/

Finding the trailhead: From Buffalo, take the New York State Thruway (I-90) east to exit 49 (Depew). At the end of the exit ramp, turn north on Transit Road (NY 78). Turn east on NY 31 and continue about 17 miles to Lockport. Turn right on NY 31, and drive 6.5 miles to Gasport Road. Turn right on Gasport and watch for the sign for Victor Fitchlee Park (Royalton Ravine). Park in the parking lot near the trailhead. GPS: N43 11.185' / W78 34.629'

The Hike

Another of the delightful, secluded places within Niagara County, Royalton Ravine—created by the flow of the

Eastern Branch of Eighteenmile Creek over thousands of years—offers a chance to view a 100-foot-deep cross section of the county's fascinating geology. Even more fun than that, however, is the bridge over the creek at the bottom of the ravine, a swaying 195-foot expanse of wooden planks suspended from cables. Safe and sturdy, the bridge nonetheless provides a sense that you're adventuring in an untamed wilderness, with the ravine's walls rising behind and in front of you and the creek's waters burbling below as you teeter your way across.

Vague trail markings and confusing combinations of blazes and nailed-up metal markers will add mystique to your hike, but it's worth sorting through them to reach this park's hidden enchantments. A short side trail takes you to the edge of the creek's wetland watershed; a steady descent leads to the bottom and the bridge; and the resulting ascent guides you to the sound of rushing water, ravine walls wet with spring runoff, and a 70-foot cascade that delivers cleansing spray to the rocks that surround it.

You can reach the cascade—appropriately named Royalton Falls—more quickly by parking on Kayner Road and taking a short trail that leads in from the road, but you'll miss the fun of the ravine descent through mature forest and the swaying footbridge, as well as the great quad workout you'll get on the ascent.

Whichever way you arrive at the falls, don't miss the ruins of a stone building that stand just before the spur trail to the cascade. Belva Lockwood, the first woman to practice law before the U.S. Supreme Court, was born in this modest homestead on the edge of the ravine in 1830. Ms. Lockwood went on to become the first woman to run for President of the United States in 1884, and again in 1888,

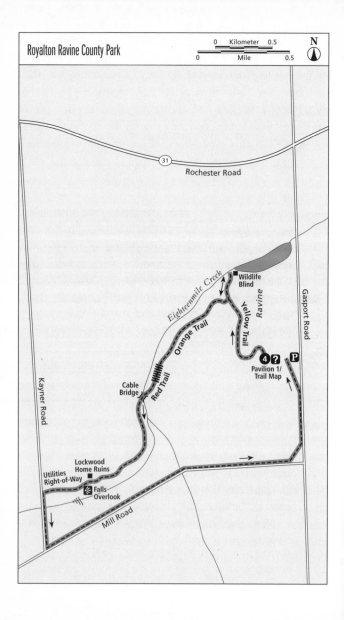

Royalton Ravine County Park

Kilometer
0   0.5

Mile
0   0.5

N

Rochester Road

31

Eighteenmile Creek

Wildlife Blind

Ravine

Yellow Trail

Orange Trail

4 ?

Pavilion 1/ Trail Map

P

Gasport Road

Cable Bridge

Red Trail

Kayner Road

Lockwood Home Ruins

Utilities Right-of-Way

Falls Overlook

Mill Road

the nominee of the short-lived Equal Rights Party. You can learn more about her at the National Women's Hall of Fame Web site, www.greatwomen.org.

Miles and Directions

0.0 Begin the trail at the end of the gravel road in the park, where you'll find a trail map displayed. Follow along the edge of the ravine/creek until you reach the woods.

0.2 Enter the woods. Follow the yellow-painted metal squares on the trees; these are the trail markers.

0.4 The yellow trail ends here, at a spot called the "wildlife blind." There's no actual blind structure, but you'll be hidden by vegetation if you want to observe wildlife in this marshy area. When you're ready, retrace your steps until you return to the intersection of the yellow and orange trails.

0.5 Turn right and continue uphill on the yellow/orange trail (it's tough to distinguish one color marker from the other, so follow both). You may see yellow or orange ribbons on trees as part of the trail markings.

0.7 The red and yellow trails meet here; continue straight. From here, painted blazes replace the metal markers for the most part. Watch for a set of steps with a yellow propylene rope as a handrail. Go down the steps.

0.8 The cable suspension bridge begins here. Cross the bridge, which is just under 200 feet long. When you're across, you'll begin a steady but gentle ascent to the top of the ravine.

1.1 Watch for the ruins of Belva Lockwood's home here. Royalton Falls is coming up on the left. Take the short trail to the left for a great view of the falls (watch your step).

1.3 You've crossed the right-of-way for high-tension wires and the county gas line, and you've reached Kayner Road. You can turn around here and retrace your steps through the ravine and back to the parking lot, or walk along the roads back to the park. The distance is about the same either way. If you're taking the road, turn left here on Kayner and walk to the next intersection.

1.5 Turn left on Mill Road. Continue to Gasport Road, and turn left.

2.3 Turn left on Gasport Road and return to the park.

2.5 You've reached the park; continue to the parking lot.

5 Buckhorn Island State Park: Long Trail

Follow along the Niagara River shoreline at the northern end of Grand Island, crossing through hardwood forest and open marshland to a slender peninsula and an expansive river view.

Distance: 4.2 miles out-and-back

Approximate hiking time: 2 hours

Difficulty: Easy

Trail surface: Old pavement / dirt path

Best season: Apr through June, Sept through Nov, winter for duck sightings

Other trail users: Cross-country skiers

Canine compatibility: Leashed dogs permitted

Fees and permits: None

Schedule: Open daily dawn to dusk

Maps: New York State Parks, http://nysparks.state.ny.us/gmaps/

Trailhead facilities: None

Trail contact: Beaver Island State Park, 2136 West Oakfield Rd., Grand Island, NY 14072; (716) 773-3271; http://nys parks.state.ny.us/parks/info .asp?parkId=21

Special considerations: Trail ices during late winter/early spring thaws

Finding the trailhead: Take I-190 to exit 20A. At the end of the exit ramp, turn east on East River Road and continue to the second Buckhorn Island parking lot (near Baseline Road) and trailhead. GPS: N43 03.550' / W78 58.163'

The Hike

The mighty Niagara River splits at the southern end of Grand Island, flowing east and west around the land and reuniting at the island's northern tip. Walking the Long Trail at Buckhorn Island State Park brings you right to the point of the river's confluence, from which you can view both the American and Canadian cities of Niagara Falls and feel the winds of Canada sweeping across the peninsula.

The trail first crosses a hardwood forest for about 0.25 mile, until the trees give way to open marshland and your first wide-open view of the Niagara River to your right. In winter, check here for overwintering ducks from the arctic regions: Canvasbacks, scaup, common goldeneye, buffleheads, mergansers, and tundra swans all gather on this open water to feed on the ready food supplies beneath the surface. Interpretive signs describe the open marsh along Woods Creek, a river tributary, just before you cross a cement bridge and continue along the river. Stop and scan this lively marsh for birds, including osprey, great blue and green herons, and other long-legged waders, as well as the very vocal sedge wrens that nest in the tussock sedge and scouring rush.

Walk under the Grand Island Bridge (part of I-190) and continue through a wooded area of trees and thick shrubs—many of which flower in spring and summer—until you reach the high tension wires and towers of the New York State Power Authority. The trail turns sharply right in about

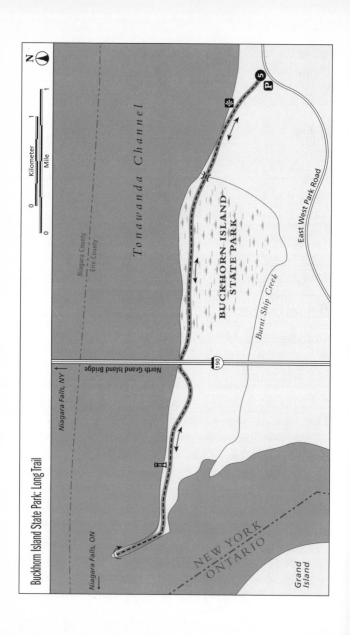

Buckhorn Island State Park: Long Trail

N

Kilometer
Mile

Niagara Falls, NY

Tonawanda Channel

Niagara County
Erie County

North Grand Island Bridge

190

Niagara Falls, ON

Niagara Falls, NY

NEW YORK
ONTARIO

Grand Island

BUCKHORN ISLAND
STATE PARK

Burnt Ship Creek

East West Park Road

5

P

100 feet, and a sign here notes that the rest of the trail is a power authority area. The trail surface becomes a grassy, undeveloped path from here, but you are welcome to walk out to the very end. With no windbreaks on either side of the peninsula, you're sure to experience some fairly intense northwesterly winds—but the view of the city of Niagara Falls, Ontario, to your left makes it worth facing into the breezes. Look closely for the cloud of river spray that rises constantly over the force of Niagara Falls. In front of you, the city of Niagara Falls, New York, stands in sharp contrast to its Ontario counterpart.

When you've had your fill of the river view and you've scanned the water's surface for interesting birds, turn around and retrace your steps back to the parking lot.

Miles and Directions

0.0 Begin the trail at the parking lot. There's only one trailhead here.

0.2 The hardwood forest ends, so you can see the Niagara River to your right. Ahead, there's an open marshland. Another trail heads off to your left; continue straight.

0.4 There's a paved loop here. Interpretive signs to the left of the loop provide information on the marshland surrounding Woods Creek. Cross the bridge and continue straight.

1.2 Cross under the North Grand Island Bridge. Don't linger under the bridge, as the cars whizzing by above you occasionally rain down gravel and other debris. In about 300 feet, the trail forks to the left and right; take the right fork. (The left fork is a paved bicycle trail.)

1.6 Pass under the high tension wires of the New York State Power Authority, well overhead.

1.8 You've reached the beginning of the peninsula. In about 250 feet, the trail turns sharply right onto the open, windswept point. A sign here reminds you that this is a New York State Power Authority area.

2.1 This is the tip of the point. To your left, the city of Niagara Falls, Ontario, surrounds the spray from one of the world's original seven natural wonders. Straight ahead, Niagara Falls, New York, rises above the water. The river expanse on either side of the point can be good territory for unusual ducks and gulls, especially in winter. When you're ready, turn around and retrace your steps to the trailhead.

4.2 Arrive back at the parking lot.

6 Niagara Falls State Park: Great Gorge Railway Trail

You've seen the falls—now see what comes next, as the rushing Niagara River cuts a spectacular dividing line between the United States and Canada.

Distance: 2.2 miles out-and-back
Approximate hiking time: 1.25 hours
Difficulty: Easy
Trail surface: Paved and gravel path
Best season: May through Oct
Other trail users: None
Canine compatibility: Leashed dogs permitted
Fees and permits: None

Schedule: Open daily dawn to dusk
Maps: Available from the Niagara Falls Gorge Discovery Center, at the trailhead
Trailhead facilities: At the Discovery Center (trailhead)
Trail contact: Regional Park Programs Office, DeVeaux Woods State Park, 3160 DeVeaux Woods Drive, Niagara Falls, NY

14305, (716) 282-5154, www
.niagarafallsstatepark.com

Special considerations: Take special care when hiking in winter.

Finding the trailhead: From Niagara Falls, take the Robert Moses Parkway north to the Niagara Gorge Discovery Center. The trailhead is behind the trailhead building, located across from the Discovery Center. GPS: N43 05.561' / W79 03.725'

The Hike

When it comes to awe-inducing power and the thrill of swirling rapids, few rivers in the northeastern United States can match the Niagara—especially in the miles after Niagara Falls tumbles from its 176-foot height into the basin below. To appreciate the river's force and its influence on the sedimentary rock walls that contain it, descend into the gorge on the gentle Great Gorge Railway Trail.

One of eight trail choices you'll find along this stretch of the river, the Great Gorge Railway Trail offers a gentle, paved slope downward, with gorge walls rising slowly but imposingly over hikers as you descend. Beginning with four excellent overlook points along the gorge rim—each with interpretive displays supplied by the park—this trail provides stunning views of the American Falls through the arch of the Rainbow Bridge, while telling stories of the falls' industrial heritage, its hospitality to flora and fauna, and its place in the nation's history.

After the fourth overlook, the trail slopes steadily but gradually downward, bringing you within touching distance of the gorge walls. Hanging gardens cling to these walls as water seeps through cracks in the dolostone, covering portions of the rock with verdant foliage in spring and summer.

In winter and early spring, look for icicles suspended like stalactites from outcroppings and ledges above.

The trail ends under the Whirlpool Bridges—two routes into Canada for cars and trains—and at a chain-link fence. Beyond the fence, the Whirlpool Rapids Trail begins, but this section is closed to the public, as the trail has not been constructed. Steep slopes make this area dangerous and impassable to hikers. To return to the gorge rim, retrace your steps up the paved trail.

Miles and Directions

0.0 Begin the trail behind the trailhead building, outside the Niagara Gorge Discovery Center. Several trails begin here. You're following Trail 4.

0.1 Here is the first overlook. An interpretive sign gives details about the concrete structure here.

0.2 Turn left at this intersection and go down the steps (or around on the ramp).

0.3 This is the second scenic overlook. To your left, you can see Niagara Falls through the Rainbow Bridge.

0.4 From the third overlook, you can see the Whirlpool Bridges and the beginning of the Whirlpool Rapids. This is a particularly good spot to view gulls and other birds.

0.5 You've begun the descent into the gorge. At this fourth overlook, you have a great view of the Whirlpool Bridges, and the interpretive display tells the story of several bridges that have spanned this river. In about 350 feet, a trail goes off to your left and behind you. This is the American Falls Gorge Trail, and it's closed to the public for maintenance. Continue straight as you descend into the gorge.

1.1 You've reached the end of the trail, under the Whirlpool Bridges and at the chain-link fence. On either side of the gorge near the bridges, you can see the foundations of a

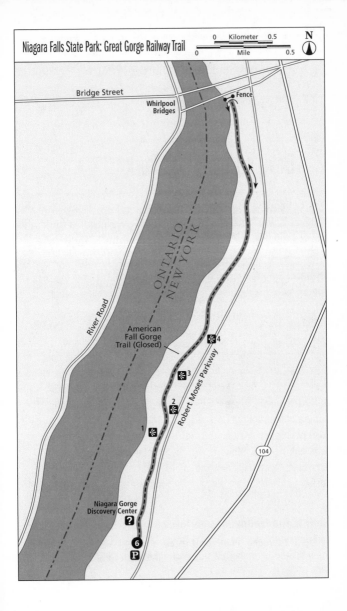

Niagara Falls State Park: Great Gorge Railway Trail

0   Kilometer   0.5

0   Mile   0.5

N

Bridge Street

Whirlpool Bridges

Fence

ONTARIO
NEW YORK

River Road

American Fall Gorge Trail (Closed)

Robert Moses Parkway

4

3

2

1

104

Niagara Gorge Discovery Center

?

6

P

former railroad bridge that preceded these steel structures. This is the end of the Great Gorge Railway Trail. Turn around and retrace your steps to the trailhead near the Discovery Center.

2.2 You are back at the Discovery Center.

7 Devil's Hole State Park

A winding descent on a 200-foot rock staircase, a trek along the Niagara River's edge, and a chance to peer inside a huge side gorge are just some of the adventures on this eventful hike.

Distance: 2.5 miles out-and-back
Approximate hiking time: 2 hours
Difficulty: Moderate
Trail surface: Gravel and dirt path, stone and concrete stairs
Best season: May through Oct
Other trail users: None
Canine compatibility: Leashed dogs permitted
Fees and permits: None
Schedule: Open daily dawn to dusk

Maps: Available from the Niagara Gorge Discovery Center, at the trailhead
Trailhead facilities: At the Discovery Center (trailhead)
Trail contact: Regional Park Programs Office, DeVeaux Woods State Park, 3160 DeVeaux Woods Drive, Niagara Falls, NY, 14305, (716) 282-5154, www .niagarafallsstatepark.com
Special considerations: Take special care when hiking in winter.

Finding the trailhead: From Niagara Falls, take the Robert Moses Parkway north past the Niagara Gorge Discovery Center to the park. The trailhead is on the left side of the parkway. GPS: N43 07.952' / W79 02.818'

The Hike

Nearly obscured from view until you're standing at its rim, the Devil's Hole area can be startling at first glimpse: a deep gouge in the Niagara Gorge—actually a side gorge, eroded by an outlet of an ancient glacial lake (long since run dry) and now filled with thriving vegetation.

You're about to follow a series of stone and concrete staircases around the perimeter of the side gorge, finally coming to ground just a few feet above water level—an extraordinary place from which to view the river's pounding rapids, standing waves, and daunting rock formations.

The steep stairs—some 300 steps in all—are only the beginning of the adventure here. This is an active gorge where rock falls are commonplace, so it's likely that the trail will be overrun in some spots by fallen dolostone and other sedimentary rock. Wear sturdy footwear with closed toes, and be prepared to step over piles of shale and sandstone as you make your way along this 1-mile trail.

If you're up to the challenge, the payoff here is rich: Viewing the river's swirling waters, still agitated from their tumble over Niagara Falls, can be one of upstate New York's sublime wilderness experiences. Rapids in this part of the river are rated Class III, but you'll see Class V white water if you continue past the Whirlpool staircase on the Whirlpool Rapids Trail.

A second set of steps awaits you at the end of the gorge portion of this hike, but these are not as steep, and they include gently inclined switchback trails between staircases. You're welcome to retrace your steps down the Devil's Hole Trail to return to your car, but I recommend climbing out of the gorge here at the end, and walking back to the trailhead along the Rim Trail at the top.

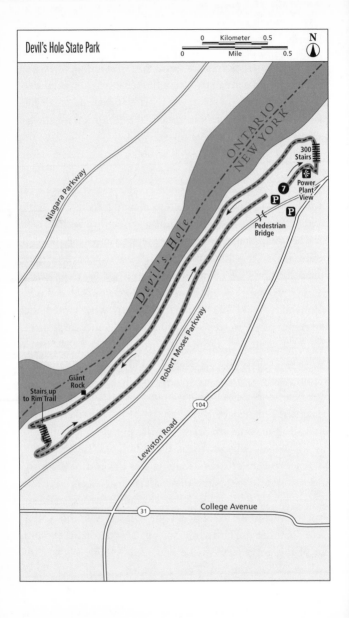

Devil's Hole State Park

N

0   Kilometer   0.5
0   Mile   0.5

ONTARIO
NEW YORK

300
Stairs

7

P

Power
Plant
View

P

Pedestrian
Bridge

Niagara Parkway

Devil's Hole

Robert Moses Parkway

Stairs up
to Rim Trail

Giant
Rock

104

Lewiston Road

31

College Avenue

Miles and Directions

0.0 If you've come up the Robert Moses Parkway from Niagara Falls, park in the area across the road from the park. Take the pedestrian walkway over the road to the gorge rim. The trailhead is to the right, near the Niagara Power Project scenic overlook. If you arrive on the parkway from the north, the park entrance is on your right.

0.3 Here are the stairs to the power plant overlook. The largest electricity producer in New York State, the recently modernized Robert Moses Niagara Power Plant diverts water from the river and into the plant, generating 2.4 million kilowatts of carbon-free electricity through the power of water. The stairs down into the gorge begin at the end of this platform.

0.5 You've come down 0.2 miles of stairs to the trail, just above water level. Turn left and begin to follow the trail along the river gorge. There are some narrow points in the trail with steep drop-offs, and some areas obscured by fallen rock. Some huge boulders seem to block the trail, but the path usually winds between them.

1.3 Here is Giant Rock, an impressive chunk of dolostone fallen from the Lockport formation above you. (From the Canadian side of the river, you can see the hole in the wall that this rock once occupied.)

1.5 Here is the Whirlpool staircase at the end of the Devil's Hole Trail. The Whirlpool Rapids Trail continues straight ahead—a challenging hike, with some boulder hopping. You are welcome to proceed down this trail to see the famous whirlpool and rapids. If you prefer, head up the stairs to the rim.

1.7 You've reached the Rim Trail. Turn left and walk along the rim to the Devil's Hole trailhead and your vehicle.

2.5 Here is the pedestrian bridge to the parking area.

8 Ellicott Creek Trailway

Meander through mowed fields on the expansive University at Buffalo North campus, and along a young memorial grove on this wide, meticulously maintained trail.

Distance: 5.2-mile shuttle
Approximate hiking time: 2 hours
Difficulty: Easy (but long)
Trail surface: Pavement
Best season: Apr through Nov
Other trail users: Cross-country skiers, joggers, bicyclists, inline skaters
Canine compatibility: Leashed dogs permitted
Fees and permits: None
Schedule: Open daily dawn to dusk
Maps: Town of Amherst, www .amherst.ny.us/pdf/highway/ bikepath.pdf
Trailhead facilities: Restrooms at parking areas at trailheads (ends of trail)
Trail contact: Town of Amherst, 5583 Main St., Williamsville, NY 14221; (716) 631-7013; www .amherst.ny.us
Special considerations: Watch out for goose droppings in spring and summer. If you are planning to walk this trail from end to end, walk with a friend and leave a second vehicle at the Ellicott Creek Park end in Tonawanda.

Finding the trailhead: Take the New York State Thruway (I-90) to exit 50, and merge onto I-290 West toward Niagara Falls. Take exit 6 (NY 324 / Sheridan Drive) and keep right at the fork. Merge onto NY 324 / Sheridan Drive, and continues for 0.7 mile to North Forest Road. Turn left on North Forest and drive 1 mile to the Ellicott Creek Trailway parking lot, on your left. GPS: N42 59.612' / W78 45.609'

To park a second car at the end of the trail, take I-290 West to exit 3 (US 62 / Niagara Falls Boulevard). Turn right at the end of the ramp, and continue 1.4 miles to Ellicott Creek Park, on your left. GPS: N43 01.511' / W78 49.320'

The Hike

This well-maintained, multiuse pathway along Ellicott Creek—a 47-mile waterway that flows from Bennington to the Niagara River—serves as a favorite fitness trail for University at Buffalo (UB) students, neighbors in Amherst and Tonawanda, and seniors living in the communities that flank the north side of the paved walkway. Whether you're looking for an energetic 5-mile hike or a short, pleasant stroll on a sunny afternoon, the Ellicott Creek Trailway is an excellent choice.

Winding but nearly entirely level, this trail wanders through UB's North Campus, skirting the man-made Lake LaSalle and the university's signature mega-dormitory, the Ellicott Complex—yet another namesake of Joseph Ellicott, the chief surveyor for the company that purchased most of the land in this area in the late 1700s. Ellicott's work helped open more than three million acres of land in this area for settlement by Europeans arriving in the 1790s, propelling Buffalo's conversion from forests and farmland into a thriving urban center.

Young trees line the trail along much of its length, each with a plaque set in the ground, bearing a dedication to a loved one whose memory is honored here. These remembrances culminate at the Amherst Memorial Hill Grove, a collection of 120 trees and a shrine walled in stone with a seating area, created in honor of Buffalo-area residents who were lost in the terrorist attacks on September 11, 2001.

Mowed fields dip away from the trail on either side along much of the creek. These fields play a significant role in the Amherst Flood Protection Project, a very effective plan to capture and divert high water in the wet seasons, defending

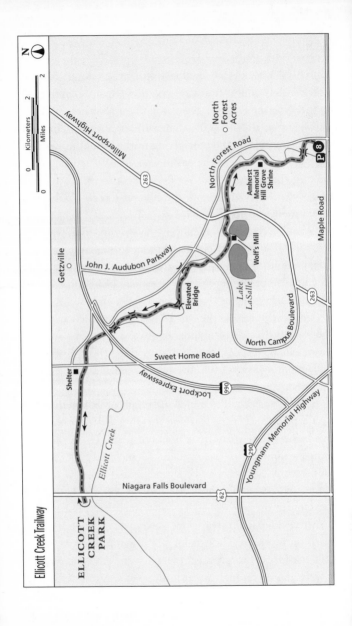

Ellicott Creek Trailway

homes and businesses along Ellicott Creek from potential flooding. Beyond the open areas, you'll see patches of wild woodland between the suburban homes as you edge along the campus. There's precious little wildlife activity here, although you may spot gray squirrels and groundhogs—and Canada geese are ubiquitous residents, sometimes sauntering across the trail in front of you with their goslings in close pursuit.

Once you leave UB's land at about the 3-mile mark, community centers and senior living developments appear to your right, giving way to office buildings and industry as Ellicott Creek intersects with the North Diversion Channel—another tool in the flooding protection system. This segment of the trail does not share the pleasing aesthetics of the first 3 miles, but the surface and surroundings are equally well-maintained, so your hike will be as comfortable as it was in the more picturesque areas. (The last 0.5-mile before Niagara Falls Boulevard can be a little mangy, as it passes through an industrial area that borders the channel on both sides.)

Miles and Directions

0.0 Begin the trail at the Ellicott Creek Trailway parking lot on North Forest Road. Walk north on the trail.

0.3 A bridge crosses the creek here.

0.5 A loop trail goes left from here. It comes back out onto the main trail in another mile. Continue straight, and enter the UB campus.

0.8 The path to the left goes to the Amherst Memorial Hill Grove shrine, which you can see from here.

1.5 The loop path rejoins the main trail here. Continue straight, and pass under the Millersport Highway bridge.

1.7 Turn left here on St. Rita Lane. You'll see a sign in front of you for Wolf's Mill, a former grist- and sawmill that once stood on this site. Cross the bridge and walk on the paved shoulder, on the right side of the road.

1.8 Turn right off the road and continue on the paved trail.

1.9 Turn right onto Frontier Road, and walk on the paved shoulder. Lake LaSalle is visible to your left, with the UB academic buildings beyond it.

2.1 Turn right on John J. Audubon Parkway. Take the trail on the right (under the bridge).

2.3 You can see a metal-and-concrete elevated bridge over the creek here to your right. Continue straight; don't turn here.

2.8 Cross a bridge over the creek as you leave the UB campus. There's an open shelter here with benches around it.

3.3 The trail diverges here; the right trail goes into a senior living community. Turn left and cross the bridge.

3.5 Here's another bridge over the creek.

3.6 I-990 passes overhead.

3.8 At this point, as the trail turns left, you're following the North Diversion Channel. Ellicott Creek continues to the southwest.

4.0 Sweet Home Road goes over the trail.

5.2 The trail ends at Niagara Falls Boulevard. If you've left a vehicle at Ellicott Creek Park, cross this busy intersection at the crosswalk. If you're doubling back on the trail, this is the turnaround point (no need to cross the street).

9 Walton Woods

Nestled behind an industrial and office complex by the same name, this charming trail system leads into old-growth forest and circles Lake Audubon on easy, paved paths.

Distance: 1.8-mile loop
Approximate hiking time: 1.25 hours
Difficulty: Easy
Trail surface: Pavement
Best season: May through Nov
Other trail users: Cross-country skiers, joggers, bicyclists, inline skaters
Canine compatibility: Leashed dogs permitted
Fees and permits: None
Schedule: Open daily dawn to dusk

Maps: Town of Amherst, www .amherst.ny.us/pdf/highway/ bikepath.pdf
Trailhead facilities: In the public library, across the parking lot from the trailhead
Trail contact: Town of Amherst, 5583 Main St., Williamsville, NY 14221; (716) 631-7013; www .amherst.ny.us
Special considerations: Sections of this trail are officially on private property, but you are welcome to walk all of the paved trails.

Finding the trailhead: Take the New York State Thruway (I-90) to exit 50, and merge onto I-290 West toward Niagara Falls. Take exit 5B (NY 263 / Millersport Highway). Continue on Millersport for 2.7 miles to Sylvan Parkway; turn left. Take Sylvan Parkway to John James Audubon Parkway; turn right on Audubon and continue to the WALTON WOODS PARK sign. Turn right and park to the right of police headquarters. The trailhead is on the right side of the parking lot (past the building). GPS: N43 01.006' / W78 46.831'

The Hike

Tucked into this fifty-two-acre parkland are such treasures as a six-acre old-growth forest with beech and tulip trees nearly two centuries old; a tranquil lake that provides sustenance to geese, ducks, and a veritable tabernacle choir of frogs; and a carpet of trillium and other wildflowers in spring and summer. In winter, the paved paths become easy cross-country ski trails, winding in and out of the woods and crossing clearings.

As you explore this little preserve, you'll find hidden playgrounds for your children's pleasure, and side trails that lead into housing developments and the Audubon New Community. You are welcome to walk on any of the paved paths around Walton Pond, or out to the adjoining streets, so long as you remain on the paths and don't wander into townhouse lawns. The map will help you stay on the main trails through the woods, whether you follow our recommended route or wander at your leisure on the winding trail. Don't feel bound to a single route, however, as wandering is part of the fun of this park. With civilization around virtually every corner, you won't get lost here; each trail brings you back to Lake Audubon or out to a road.

Miles and Directions

0.0   Begin the trail at the parking lot behind the police headquarters.

0.1   Leave the developed area and enter the woods on the paved path. In a few feet, the path comes to a T intersection. Go left along Lake Audubon.

0.3   A path into a housing development goes left. Go straight.

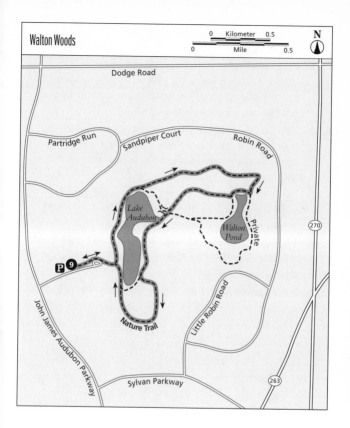

0.4 Bear right, around Lake Audubon. In a moment, a path to a playground goes to the right. Stop at the playground if you like, or continue straight.

0.8 The trail goes straight and to the right here. The straight trail continues through the woods and skirts a housing development. Continue straight, toward Walton Pond. In about 250 feet, turn right and continue around the west side of the pond.

0.9 Bear right or left on the paved path; both will bring you back to Lake Audubon in about the same amount of time.

1.1 The trail forks right and left here. The left fork takes you toward the Nature Trail, a dirt path through the old-growth forest. To the right, there's a bridge and a return to the path you took along Lake Audubon. Go left.

1.3 Here's another fork in the trail. Go left, toward the Nature Trail. In about 200 feet, the trail goes straight and to the right. The straight trail goes into a housing complex and out to Sylvan Parkway. Turn right.

1.5 The Nature Trail—a dirt path to the right—begins here. If you'd like to see the old-growth woods up close, turn right. To stay on the paved path, continue straight.

1.6 Cross the bridge over this water source. The trail straight ahead returns you to the parking lot. Turn left at the next intersection.

1.8 You've arrived back at the parking lot.

10 Akron Falls Park: Conservation Trail

This easy amble along Murder Creek in Akron begins with a waterfall viewpoint, and continues on the edge line between developed land and wilderness.

Distance: 2 miles out-and-back
Approximate hiking time: 1 hour
Difficulty: Easy
Trail surface: Old pavement / dirt path
Best season: Apr through Nov
Other trail users: Cross-country skiers, joggers, bicyclists
Canine compatibility: Leashed dogs permitted
Fees and permits: None

Schedule: Open daily dawn to dusk
Maps: *National Geographic Topo! New York State edition*
Trailhead facilities: At Cummings Lodge on Skyline Road
Trail contact: Erie County Parks and Recreation, 95 Franklin St., Room 1359, Buffalo, NY 14202; (716) 858-8355; www.erie.gov/parks

Finding the trailhead: From Buffalo, take I-90 east to exit 49 (Depew). At the end of the ramp, turn left at Transit Road / NY 78. In 1.3 miles, turn right onto Main Street (NY 5). Continue 10 miles to NY 93 / Buell Street, and turn left. Turn right at East Skyline Drive, and continue straight into the park. Park your car at Cummings Lodge (the big stone lodge building on your left), where the trail begins. N43 00.912' / W78 29.104'

The Hike

If you don't live in northeastern Erie County, you may never have come across this agreeable little park on the banks of Murder Creek. Legend has it that in the early 1800s, several murders took place here in a single night: A family became

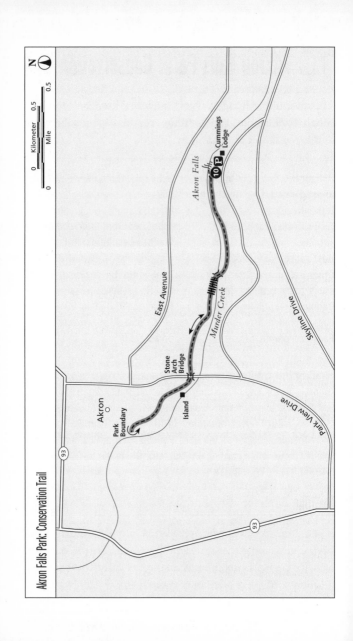

Akron Falls Park: Conservation Trail

unsuspecting victims of a desperate officer named Sanders, an Indian man named Gray Wolf died defending a young native woman from this crazed officer, and Sanders died of wounds inflicted by Gray Wolf. The story differs depending on who tells it, but the event gave the creek its name.

Here the creek splits the park into two distinct territories: the mowed, developed side with playgrounds, baseball diamonds, and picnic areas, and the wilder side with its ample crops of ferns, moss, and hardwood forest. This easy walk allows you to enjoy both regions.

From the parking lot, descend a set of once-paved steps to the landing. To your right about 100 feet, the falls that give this park its name flow with gusto from the stony cliff at its highest point. Depending on the season, you may see a raging torrent of greenish water and churning foam, or a soothing trickle cascading serenely over the precipice. Go in early spring or in autumn to see the falls at their most exciting.

As you turn away from the falls, you'll follow the orange blazes that mark the Conservation Trail, a 177-mile hiking trail that connects the Finger Lakes Trail—part of the North Country National Scenic Trail in southern New York State—to the Bruce Trail in Canada. With its origins reaching back to 1961, the Conservation Trail passes through many state and county parks in Cattaraugus, Wyoming, Genesee, Erie, and Niagara counties. If you're motivated to do so, you can walk from Akron Falls to Niagara Falls on this trail, or all the way south to Allegany State Park.

Pass through the hardwood forest of American beech, butternut hickory, black walnut, red and Scotch pine, and Norway spruce, among others, with the creek to your right. The trail crosses a bridge that straddles the creek and continues on the developed side of the park, where the creek becomes a lake created by the dam you see ahead. Built as a Works Progress Administration project in 1933, the dam was one of several projects completed during the Great Depression's federal job creation program. The stone and pavement steps and the first section of trail also resulted from this sweeping effort, designed to improve public spaces throughout America.

Miles and Directions

0.0 Begin the trail at the parking lot at Cummings Lodge. There's only one trailhead here; walk down the steps and turn right at the bottom, toward the sound of falling water.

0.1 Here is Akron Falls. This overlook is a great place for photos. When you're ready, turn around and walk back past the steps, and begin following the orange blazes.

0.3 You're walking along Murder Creek. Back and to your left, a closed road comes down from the top of the cliff. Continue straight, following the orange blazes.

0.5 To your right, a bridge crosses the creek. Cross here and take the stairs to your left immediately after crossing the bridge. Continue west along this side of the creek. Here the creek becomes a man-made lake, created by the dam up ahead.

0.8 You've reached a stone arch bridge. You can see the creek/ lake water cascading down over the dam into the creek below. Walk through the portal in the bridge (you'll see the orange blazes here). In about 350 feet, you'll pass a bridge on your left that leads onto an island in the creek, with a developed picnic area. Continue past this (or stop, if you like).

1.0 This three-ton bridge marks the boundary of Akron Falls Park. The trail continues to Niagara Falls, but if you'd only planned to walk this park today, this is your turnaround point. Walk back to the parking lot on the same path.

2.0 You've arrived back at the parking lot.

11 Iroquois National Wildlife Refuge: Swallow Hollow Trail

There's no better place to hear the amphibious spring chorus than in this emergent marsh, where frogs thrive among the cattails and reeds and waterfowl gather on the still waters.

Distance: 1.3-mile loop
Approximate hiking time: 40 minutes
Difficulty: Easy
Trail surface: Boardwalk, gravel, and some dirt path
Best season: Apr through June, Sept and Oct
Other trail users: Birders, snowshoers, and cross-country skiers
Canine compatibility: Leashed dogs permitted
Fees and permits: None

Schedule: Open daily dawn to dusk
Maps: Iroquois National Wildlife Refuge, www.fws.gov/northeast/iroquois/
Trailhead facilities: None
Trail contact: Iroquois National Wildlife Refuge, 1101 Casey Rd., Basom, NY 14013; (585) 948-5445; www.fws.gosv/northeast/iroquois/
Special considerations: As in all wetlands, wear insect repellent in warm weather.

Finding the trailhead: Take the New York State Thruway (I-90) east to exit 48A (Pembroke). At the end of the exit ramp, turn left on Allegheny Road, and continue to Lewiston Road. Turn right on Lewiston and take the next left, Knowlesville Road. Continue north on Knowlesville until you reach the parking lot for Swallow Hollow Trail, on your left. GPS: N43 07.541' / W78 19.527'

The Hike

You'll want to linger on this easy trail for longer than its length would suggest, especially if you love seeing and hearing spring peepers and other vocal frogs and toads. The protected marshland and slowly moving waters within this part of the national refuge offer prime habitat for amphibians, as well as feeding and breeding ground for ducks and other water-loving birds. Acadian flycatchers live and breed here, as do the beautiful red-headed woodpecker and Virginia rail, a swamp dweller that's fairly common, but often hard to glimpse (try visiting just before sunset).

The trail passes through three distinct habitats: a forested wetland, the emergent marsh you'll traverse by boardwalk and man-made dike, and an upland hardwood forest that begins as the land rises about 2 feet above the waterline. This concentration of ecosystems in one small area makes for terrific wildlife viewing: Watch for muskrat and snapping turtles in the marsh, white-tailed deer in the woods, and hawks over the wetland to the left of the dike.

Once you've seen this tiny sliver of the 10,828-acre refuge, you're sure to want to explore more of this lovely place. The Kanyoo Trail (1.2-mile loop), on the southern side of the refuge near the headquarters on Casey Road, offers more expansive views of open fields and vernal pools, with an observation platform over the wetlands. The Onondaga Trail (1.2 miles each way) follows a gravel dike straight into mature woodland to a loop around a quiet pond. Overlooks within the refuge on NY 77 and NY 63 offer opportunities to set up a scope for hawk and waterfowl sightings, especially in spring and fall when the refuge becomes an important stopover site for migrating flocks. Tundra swans, grebes, many duck species, and the ubiquitous Canada geese rest and feed here before moving on to breeding grounds to the north, or to warmer climates to the south.

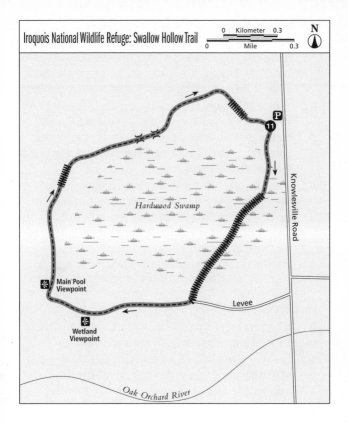

Hardwood Swamp

Main Pool Viewpoint

Wetland Viewpoint

Knowlesville Road

Levee

Oak Orchard River

Miles and Directions

0.0 Begin the trail at the parking lot. Take the wooden stairs/ramp and begin the trail to the left.

0.1 You're crossing a forested wetland, with several vantage points from which to view open water surrounded by trees, many with their roots submerged. This is a good place to look for wood ducks, which breed in this area.

0.3 The boardwalk ends at the gravel path on the levee. Turn right to continue the loop. You may want to detour to the left to scan the vegetation to the right of the levee for warblers, and to check for frogs and turtles along the waterway here. When you're ready, continue from the boardwalk to the right.

0.5 The interpretive sign here reminds us to stop to view the wetland to the left of the trail. This is a good place to look for hunting hawks and turkey vultures soaring over the open area, and to listen for red-winged blackbirds and other birds that perch on reeds and cattails.

0.6 This is a particularly choice spot to stop and listen to the frogs, and to view the emergent marsh. Look for herons standing and watching for fish in the nearly still water. In about 250 feet, the gravel trail enters the woods, and gradually becomes a dirt path. With just a couple of feet in elevation change, the trees shift to maple, tulip tree, cherry, and beech. Tight concentrations of evergreens signal plantations. Short sections of boardwalk cross over lower, wetter portions of the trail.

0.9 A dirt path goes left here, into a patch of evergreens. The path just dead-ends in a few feet. Continue straight.

1.2 You've reached the boardwalk that leads back to the parking lot and the end of the trail. The land dips down just enough to become forested wetland once again.

1.3 Here is the parking lot.

12 Reinstein Woods Nature Preserve: History, Beech Tree, Footprint, and Lily Pond Trails Loop

Meticulously preserved and protected by its original owner, this sparkling preserve's trails lead to open meadows, ponds covered with water lilies, bird-filled marshland, and eighty acres of ancient forest.

Distance: 1.7-mile loop

Approximate hiking time: 1 hour

Difficulty: Easy

Trail surface: Mowed path with some boardwalk, dirt in some sections

Best season: Apr through Nov

Other trail users: Cross-country skiers

Canine compatibility: No pets allowed

Fees and permits: None

Schedule: Trails are open daily dawn to dusk

Maps: New York State Depart-ment of Environmental Con-servation, www.dec.ny.gov/education/1837.html

Trailhead facilities: At the Edu-cation Center as you enter the preserve, open Mon–Fri 9 a.m.–5 p.m., Sat 1–4 p.m., closed Sun.

Trail contact: Reinstein Woods Nature Preserve, 93 Honorine Dr., Depew, NY 14043; (716) 683-5959; www.dec.ny.gov/education.1837.html

Special considerations: No bicycles allowed; wear insect repellent in wet seasons.

Finding the trailhead: From Buffalo, take the New York State Thruway (I-90) east to exit 49 (Depew). At the end of the ramp, turn right at Transit Road / NY 78. Turn right (west) onto Como Park Boulevard, and continue 1.1 miles to Honorine Drive. Turn left onto

Honorine. The entrance gate to the preserve is on your left, at 93 Honorine Dr. GPS: N42 53.467' / W78 43.075'

The Hike

If you've ever wondered what the upstate New York land-scape looked like before the Europeans arrived and started clear-cutting the forests, there's a sliver of untouched, ancient land that still remains—thanks, in part, to a visionary physician who bought up this land in the 1930s to preserve it in perpetuity.

Dr. Victor Reinstein was a man of uncommon capability and generosity, serving his community as an attorney as well as a physician, and making major gifts as well, not the least of which was this personal estate. When he died in 1984, he left instructions that the land be preserved, and New York State agreed to do so—and, in 1991, his widow, Julia Reinstein, expanded the Reinstein Woods State Nature Preserve with an additional gift.

Today, we can rejoice in the treasure this family left us, from Lily Pond—which blooms with bright pink water lilies in spring and summer—to the Champion Beech Tree, a massive American beech that in 2001 measured an astonishing 11 feet, 3.5 inches around (so it's even larger now). It's not often that we see a tree of this girth and height (103 feet) east of the Sequoia redwood forests, so this is a rare treat indeed.

Between the startlingly beautiful ponds, the huge trees, and the nodding cattails in the marshlands, Reinstein Woods offers a smattering of education. Our walk begins on the History Trail, where you can read about some of Dr. Reinstein's efforts to preserve the estate's natural wonders and restore some others; later along the trail, the State Symbols

Trail provides some surprising facts about New York State. (Did you know we have a State Fish and a State Fossil?)

Whenever you visit, be sure to bring your binoculars. Reinstein Woods's multiple habitats attract a fine variety of birds, especially in spring and fall as the warblers and other songbirds move through. Wildlife here ranges from white-tailed deer and coyote to squirrels and rabbits, and both snapping and painted turtles can be found along the edges of the ponds.

The loop described here takes you around the perimeter of the preserve, where you'll pass through every habitat and achieve a full overview of the preserve. Plan some extra time at this preserve, because once you've completed the loop, you'll want to go back and explore the ponds, the woods, or the marshland more thoroughly on the cross trails.

Miles and Directions

0.0 At the parking lot, walk to the kiosk with the trail map. Take the brick path to the beginning of the dirt path, passing the visitor center and other buildings on your left. The trail begins as you pass the gazebo on your right. Take the History Trail.

0.1 Continue straight as the Footprint and Beech Tree Trails go left. Stay on the History Trail.

0.3 There's a closed trail ahead. Some areas of the preserve are closed to the public for continued research and preservation work. Turn left and continue on the History Trail.

0.5 You're at Flattail Lake. The Footprint and History Trails join here. Continue to the right on the History Trail, around Mallard Meadow.

0.7 Part of the Beech Tree Trail goes off to the left. Continue straight.

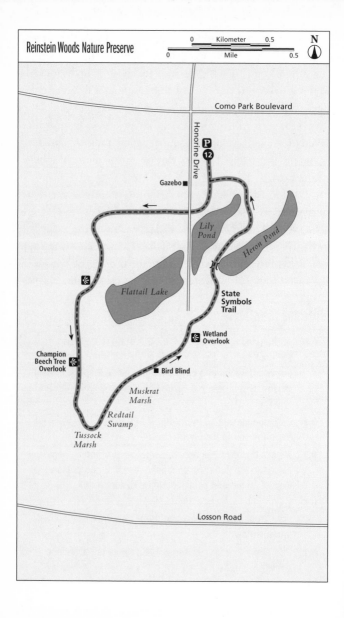

Reinstein Woods Nature Preserve

Kilometer 0.5

Mile 0.5

N

Como Park Boulevard

Honorine Drive

P 12

Gazebo ■

Lily Pond

Heron Pond

Flattail Lake

State Symbols Trail

Wetland Overlook

Champion Beech Tree Overlook

Bird Blind

Muskrat Marsh

Redtail Swamp

Tussock Marsh

Losson Road

0.8 Here is Champion Beech Tree Overlook. Stop here to see this magnificent, old-growth American beech tree. From here, proceed straight ahead on Beech Tree Trail, through Tussock Marsh.

1.1 Beech Tree Trail continues left. Go straight ahead through Redtail Swamp and Muskrat Marsh, to the Footprint Trail. When the trail splits in about 400 feet, continue straight. There's a bird blind looking out over the marsh to your right; this is a great place to stop and look for waterfowl and long-legged waders.

1.3 This is an excellent place to view the entire wetland. In about 200 feet, you'll begin the State Symbols Trail. Turn right; the Footprint Trail continues straight.

1.4 You've reached Heron Pond. Bear left and join the Lily Pond Trail. In about 100 feet, turn right and cross the bridge between Heron and Lily Ponds.

1.7 Here is the visitor center, where you can use the restroom, get water, and stop in the bookstore/gift shop.

13 Tillman Road Wildlife Management Area

Scan a cattail marsh for migrating waterfowl from an observation platform, cross a hardwood forest, and walk along the edge of an open wetland—all in just 235 acres.

Distance: 2.2-mile loop and side trail

Approximate hiking time: 1.25 hours

Difficulty: Easy

Trail surface: Mowed path with some boardwalk, dirt in some sections

Best season: Apr through Nov

Other trail users: Cross-country skiers, birders

Canine compatibility: Leashed dogs permitted

Fees and permits: None

Schedule: Open daily dawn to dusk.

Maps: *National Geographic Topo! New York State* edition

Trailhead facilities: None

Trail contact: New York State Department of Environmental Conservation, 270 Michigan Ave., Buffalo NY 14203; (716) 851-7010; www.dec.ny.gov/outdoor/9166.html

Special considerations: Trails can be muddy in spring and after rains. Wear insect repellent in wet seasons.

Finding the trailhead: From Buffalo, take I-90 east to exit 49 (Depew). At the end of the ramp, turn left at Transit Road / NY 78. Turn right onto Main Street (NY 5), and drive to Ransom Road in Clarence. Turn right on Ransom and continue to Tillman Road. Turn right on Tillman, and drive to the parking lot for Tillman Road WMA, on your left before Shisler Road. GPS: N42 57.595' / W78 36.629'

The Hike

Residents of Clarence keep mum about this sweet little preserve, concealed between housing developments and away from the bustle of Main Street to the north and the Thruway to the south. Even with the relative secrecy, however, all manner of waterfowl find their way here during spring and fall migration, pulling in after a long flight to rest and recharge on the nutrient-rich waters of the area's eighty-acre cattail marsh.

Two parking areas serve this refuge; the more-popular parking at the corner of Shisler and Bergtold Roads connects visitors quickly with the boardwalk and viewing platform over the marsh. We've chosen to begin this hike at the other parking lot off of Tillman Road, with the marsh-viewing area as a bonus trail at the end of the hike. You'll discover the entire interlocking ecosystem here, from the woods and meadow to the low wetland, before reaching a ground-level viewpoint of the cattail marsh from Tillman Road—which will whet your appetite for a higher perspective from the boardwalk and platform.

Birders will find more than Canada geese and mallards here, especially during migration. Wood ducks breed in the marsh, and great blue and green herons, pied-billed grebes, Virginia rails, soras, and American bitterns have all been spotted in season. The woods and wetland attract songbirds as well, so be sure to walk this trail in May for the greatest variety of warblers, vireos, sparrows, and other passerines.

The loudest spring chorus, however, comes from the frogs: Seven species thrive here, including spring peepers, green, wood, bull, Western chorus, Northern leopard, and gray tree frogs. Salamanders also live here—they're most easily seen at dawn and dusk—and the edges of the marsh are favorite grounds for painted turtles. Watch for garter and northern water snakes near the larger bodies of water. In summer, the meadow and marsh fill with butterflies, with mourning cloaks emerging as early as late March's first warm days.

Mammals are harder to see among the reeds and in the forest's thick shrubs and understory, but keep an eye out for muskrat, mink, beaver, and raccoon, as well as the more common white-tailed deer, gray squirrel, and eastern cottontail.

Miles and Directions

0.0 The trail begins at the southeast side of the parking lot. Several trails begin here, but they all loop back to this spot. Walk straight (south) into the woods. The trail bears left shortly.

0.2 The path emerges in a clearing, and continues in the woods to the left. To the right, a high signpost indicates the Edge Trail and the Meadow Trail. This is the only signpost in the preserve. The Meadow Trail loops around to the right and back to the parking lot. Go straight here to continue on the Edge Trail.

0.3 A bridge goes over a wet area here. In about 350 feet, the trail reaches a boundary with private land. Bear left on the trail, around the edge of the marshland. The marsh becomes more visible as you continue toward a boardwalk.

0.4 The boardwalk begins here. It goes up to a viewing platform, from which you can see across the marsh. When you're ready, walk down the other side of the boardwalk and continue on the trail.

0.7 A path to the right goes out to the road from here. You can see a gravel path across the road—that's a private driveway.

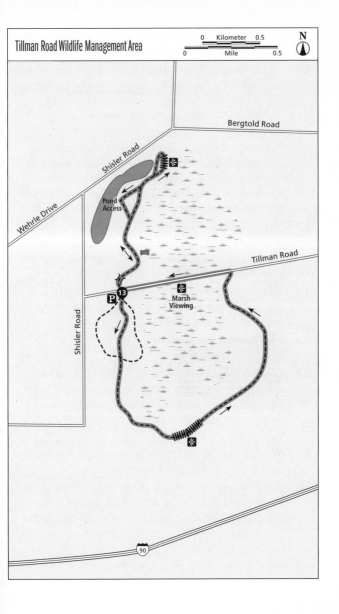

Tillman Road Wildlife Management Area

0 Kilometer 0.5
0 Mile 0.5

N

Bergtold Road

Shisler Road

Wehrle Drive

Pond Access

Tillman Road

Shisler Road

P 13

Marsh Viewing

90

Continue straight on the trail. In about 200 feet, a path goes off to the left. Continue straight.

0.8 The path begins to curve to the left here. A path to the right goes out to the road; continue to bear left. In about 300 feet, the path that went off to the left a moment ago emerges again, connecting with the main trail.

1.0 The trail ends at Tillman Road. Turn left to walk back to the parking lot and your car. To the right, the marsh comes into view; this is a great place to observe waterfowl and long-legged waders through binoculars. While traffic is light on this country road, be careful to choose a safe position from which to view the marsh.

1.3 You've reached the parking lot. You can end your hike here, or turn right, cross Tillman Road, and continue to the north. This trail begins as a bridge crosses the waterway. Cross the bridge and turn right at the first intersection.

1.4 You've reached a wide clearing with a bench. Bear left and continue on the trail, crossing two small bridges over wet areas. Turn right as the trail turns.

1.5 A trail goes left here. Continue straight; you'll take the left trail on your way back.

1.7 Go up the five steps you see here to the raised boardwalk. Turn right and walk out to the viewing platform. When you're ready to continue, walk down the steps at the platform to the return trail, turn left onto the trail, and begin your walk back.

1.8 When you reach the first intersection, bear right. This part of the trail follows the edge of a large pond.

1.9 You can access the pond here by following the trail through the reeds and shrubs to the water's edge. When you're ready, come back up the pond access trail and bear right on the path. In about 350 feet, turn right onto the trail and walk back to Tillman Road.

2.2 You've reached Tillman Road. Cross the road to return to the parking lot.

14 Hunter's Creek County Park

Trek through a wild, undeveloped park with a plunging ravine, a merrily babbling creek, and wide woodlands filled with northern hardwoods.

Distance: 1.9-mile loop
Approximate hiking time: 1.25 hours
Difficulty: Easy
Trail surface: Dirt path
Best season: Apr through Nov
Other trail users: Scouts, orienteering groups
Canine compatibility: Leashed dogs permitted
Fees and permits: None
Schedule: Open daily dawn to dusk
Maps: The best is on the Western New York Mountain Bicycling Association Web site: www.wnymba.org/static/maps/hunters.pdf
Trailhead facilities: None
Trail contact: Erie County Parks and Recreation, 95 Franklin St., Room 1359, Buffalo, NY 14202; (716) 858-8355; www.erie.gov/parks
Special considerations: Trails can be muddy in spring and after rains. Wear insect repellent in wet seasons.

Finding the trailhead: From Buffalo, take I-90 West to exit 54. Merge onto NY 400 South, and drive 13 miles to the US 20A exit. Keep left and follow the signs to Warsaw. Turn right at Strykersville Road, and in 1 mile, turn right on Hunter's Creek Road. Continue on Hunter's Creek to Centerline Road, and turn right. The parking area is on the right in about 0.5 mile. GPS: N42 44.219' / W78 33.072'

The Hike

A relatively new acquisition by Erie County, Hunter's Creek Park (originally named Sergeant Mark Rademacher Park) remains happily undeveloped, with a single sign at its simple parking lot. Outdoor enthusiasts know that this means a more authentic wilderness experience than we may find at more sophisticated parks—and indeed, the winding trails lead through thick stands of mature hardwoods and scattered evergreens, along an exuberant creek, and up and down the ridgeline along a natural ravine.

Scout troops and orienteering clubs make frequent use of this park, so trails are well marked and maintained, and numbered intersection signs help you find your way through the woods. More than fifteen trails lead through the park, so there are many intersections; the trail described here provides a roundabout overview of the park's most interesting features. Once you've been to this little-known gem, you're sure to return to explore other trails or to follow the Conservation Trail—a project of the Finger Lakes Trail Conference—as a through-hike from the southern end of the park to its northern boundary.

As lovely as this park is in any season, spring may be its most exciting time, when the creek runs high and wildflowers fill the forest floor with pockets of bright blooms. Keep an eye out for trees that bear spectacular holes, some of which may house nesting pileated woodpeckers. You'll hear the tap-tap-tap of bill against tree trunk just about anywhere in the park.

Miles and Directions

0.0 The trail begins at the east end of the parking lot. You'll see two trails beginning here; take the one on the left. The trails are not blazed until you actually enter the woods, but you'll see a tree with three pink dots. This is the beginning of the pink trail, which you will follow on this hike. At the double

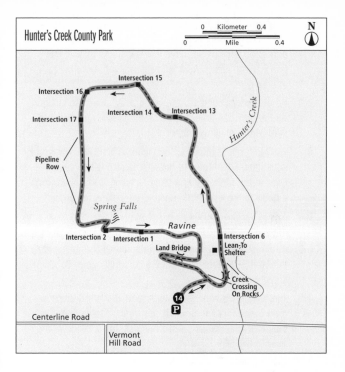

Hunter's Creek County Park

Intersection 15

Intersection 16

Intersection 14   Intersection 13

Intersection 17

Hunter's Creek

Pipeline Row

Spring Falls

Ravine

Intersection 2   Intersection 1

Intersection 6
Lean-To Shelter

Land Bridge

Creek Crossing On Rocks

14
P

Centerline Road

Vermont Hill Road

0   Kilometer   0.4

0   Mile   0.4

N

pink blaze at Intersection 10, turn left. (The Sergeant Mark trail is blazed with gold and green chevrons; it goes right here.)

0.1 A spur trail (marked with pink dots) goes right here. Continue straight. You're heading down into the ravine on a gentle slope. In about 130 feet, a bridge crosses the creek. The trail begins to follow the creek through the woods.

0.2 Cross the creek here by stepping on the rocks. In about 150 feet, the yellow trail begins. You can see a lean-to shelter on a hill a little way down the yellow trail. Continue on the pink trail.

0.3 At the top of this hill, several trails intersect. The red trail goes straight, the Sergeant Mark trail goes left and right, and pink goes left. Turn left. In a few steps, turn right at Intersection 6. From here, you're following a ridge above the ravine to your right.

0.6 Here at Intersection 13, the blue trail appears. Go straight on the pink trail. In about 150 feet, cross a dirt road and step over a drainage ditch.

0.7 You're at Intersection 14. The blue trail goes left, while pink goes right. Follow pink to the right. Watch out for a subsidence in the path, where a tree has fallen. You'll need to go around to the left of the tree and the hole in the ground.

0.8 At Intersection 15, the pink and yellow trails meet once again. Turn left on the pink trail.

0.9 At Intersection 16, turn left. (An unmarked trail goes right.) In about 200 feet, you'll join the blue trail again. Continue straight.

1.0 The trail emerges here at Intersection 17, at a dirt access road called Pipeline Row. There's a picnic table here. The blue trail goes straight, while the pink trail turns down the road to the right.

1.2 The Sergeant Mark trail crosses the road here. Continue straight. In about 250 feet, you'll see a sign for the Spring Falls Trail, which is blazed purple. Turn left and follow the purple blazes for a side trip to the falls, which you'll find in about 150 feet. These merry little stair-step falls continue down the creek to a trail intersection.

1.3 The purple and yellow trails meet here and cross the creek. Step across on the boulders. From here, you'll continue uphill along the other side of the creek, with even nicer views of the falling water. The purple and pink trails join in a moment at Intersection 2; rejoin the pink trail and turn right.

1.4 At Intersection 1, the yellow trail goes left and pink goes right. Take the right trail. Be sure to stop and enjoy the ravine view along this stretch.

1.7 You'll see an unmarked trail to the left that crosses this creek tributary on a narrow path. You can take this shortcut path if you like, or continue straight to cross the creek and return to the parking area.

1.8 Cross the creek (it's a little tricky here, with access downhill and back up on the other side). Turn right on the pink trail after you've crossed.

1.9 You've arrived back at the trailhead and your vehicle.

15 Emery Park

The developed areas in this park mask its true beauty: a ravine carved by Cazenovia Creek, with two cascading waterfalls easily reached on a woodland trail.

Distance: 2.2-mile loop

Approximate hiking time: 1 hour

Difficulty: Easy

Trail surface: Dirt path covered in woodland detritus

Best season: July through Oct

Other trail users: Cross-country skiers

Canine compatibility: Leashed dogs permitted

Fees and permits: None

Schedule: Open daily dawn to dusk

Maps: *National Geographic Topo! New York State* edition

Trailhead facilities: Restrooms and running water at field house in park

Trail contact: Erie County Parks and Recreation, 95 Franklin St., Room 1359, Buffalo, NY 14202; (716) 858-8355; www.erie.gov/parks

Special considerations: Trail can be very muddy in wet seasons

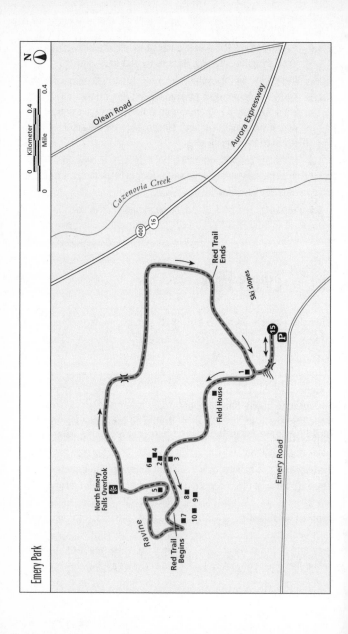

Emery Park

North Emery
Falls Overlook

Ravine

Red Trail
Begins

Field House

Red Trail
Ends

Ski slopes

Emery Road

Cazenovia Creek

Olean Road

Aurora Expressway

400
16

N

Kilometer   0   0.4

Mile   0   0.4

P
15

1
2
3
4
5
6
7
8
9
10

Finding the trailhead: From Buffalo, take I-190 South and merge onto I-90 West. Take exit 54 toward NY 16 / West Seneca / East Aurora, and merge onto NY 400. In 17 miles, NY 400 becomes NY 16 (Olean Road). Continue on 16 to Emery Road and turn right. The park is on the right in about 0.8 mile. GPS: N42 42.921' / W78 35.556'

The Hike

A favorite park for cross-country and downhill skiing and snowboarding, Emery Park attracts families throughout the winter, making this southern-tier park's motorized lifts and groomed slopes especially popular when the snows pile up. When winter ends, families return to picnic in the pavilions and play games on the mowed lawns, some never venturing into the cool green woods beyond.

Yet it's in these woods that Emery's deeper secret lies: A beautiful ravine, sculpted over thousands of years by Cazenovia Creek, features a relaxed, free-flowing, 30-foot cascade known as North Emery Falls. Another waterfall— the 40-foot Emery Falls—greets visitors as they cross the bridge from the parking area into the park's developed section. Before you turn up your nose at the mowed lawns and the number of pavilions, note that the vast majority of these buildings have been here since before 1935, and some were part of the Town of Aurora's land purchase from Helen B. Emery back in 1925, when the park's first 175 acres were opened for public enjoyment.

We've chosen a route that uses the park's road to take you to the official trailhead, forming a loop around the park's northern section that brings you to both waterfalls.

Emery holds enough charms to attract nature lovers here at any time of year. Wildflowers cover the forest floor beginning in late April, and the mature woods contain many of the northern hardwoods and evergreens that lend their color and fragrance to the atmosphere in spring and summer.

You may see that the ravine is rimmed with orange caution fencing. This is a temporary measure while the county explores options for bridge repairs and a permanent railing system.

Miles and Directions

0.0 Begin at the parking lot. Walk left to the bridge over Cazenovia Creek. You'll have a good view of Emery Falls as you cross the bridge. Walk up the park road and follow the road to the left, past the field house and toward Pavilion 7.

0.6 Behind Pavilion 7, you can see the first trail sign: a red blaze outlined by a blue arrow. From here, the trail seems to go left and right. The left trail continues to the creek, but the blazes end after the creek (and there's no bridge here). You'll see the red blazes on trees going right. Follow the blazes.

0.9 Here the trail leads to the crossing of a creek tributary and ravine. This may be closed at times; if you can't cross here, bear right around the tributary until it disappears into a drainage pipe under solid ground. Turn left there, and follow the tributary back to the trail. Continue right.

1.1 From here, you have an excellent view of North Emery Falls.

1.4 Cross a bridge over a stream here. Continue to follow the red blazes through the woods.

1.8 The red blazes have led you to the road. Turn right here (90 degrees—there's also a 180-degree turn to the right, but don't take it) and walk up the road to the next picnic pavilion.

2.1 Just beyond the pavilion, you'll find the bridge you crossed over Emery Falls at the beginning of the hike. Cross it again to return to the parking lot.

2.2 Here is the parking lot.

16 Chestnut Ridge Park: Eternal Flame Trail

A flame powered by a natural gas source in a grotto behind a waterfall: What could be more intriguing? Find your way down the gorge and up the creek to witness this fascinating phenomenon.

Distance: 1.4 miles out-and-back
Approximate hiking time: 1 hour
Difficulty: Moderate
Trail surface: Dirt path and creek bed
Best season: July through Oct
Other trail users: None
Canine compatibility: Leashed dogs permitted
Fees and permits: None
Schedule: Open daily dawn to dusk
Maps: *National Geographic Topo! New York State* edition

Trailhead facilities: None
Trail contact: Erie County Parks and Recreation, 95 Franklin St., Room 1359, Buffalo, NY 14202; (716) 858-8355; www.erie.gov/ parks
Special considerations: Spring snowmelt and rains can swell the creek and increase the current, making this hike much more difficult. Wear waterproof footwear and bring a walking stick in spring.

Finding the trailhead: Take the New York State Thruway (I-90) west to exit 55 (US 219 / Orchard Park). From US 219, take the Armor Duells Road exit toward NY 277. Keep right and merge onto Armor Duells Road. Turn right at Chestnut Ridge Road, and continue past the park to Seufert Road. Turn right on Seufert and park at the trailhead. GPS: N42 42.003' / W78 45.145'

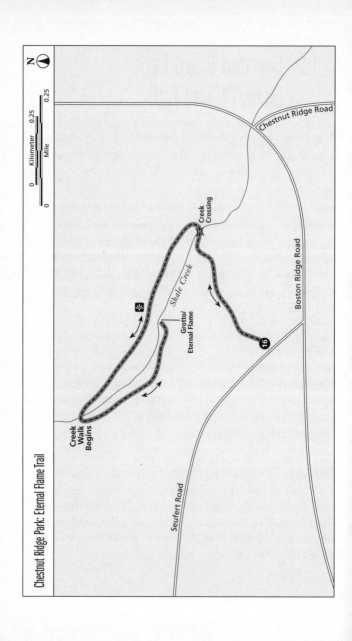

Chestnut Ridge Park: Eternal Flame Trail

Creek Walk Begins

Shale Creek

Grotto/Eternal Flame

Creek Crossing

16

Seufert Road

Boston Ridge Road

Chestnut Ridge Road

N

0   Kilometer   0.25

0   Mile   0.25

The Hike

If Erie County Parks and Recreation decided to choose a signature hike—a trail that provided the most unusual and gratifying outdoor experience in the area—the Eternal Flame Trail at Chestnut Ridge Park might qualify. In just 0.75 of a mile, this hike descends through a tranquil hardwood forest into a deep ravine sliced out of the rock by Shale Creek, then crisscrosses the creek itself on whatever rocks and logs may have landed here during the area's legendary storms. This eventful hike leads to one of the area's best-kept secrets: A 4-inch flame, fueled by underground natural gas, rising through tiny cracks in the earth.

You'll find this flame in a grotto beside the aptly named Eternal Flame Falls—a pleasantly tumbling trickle in the drier summer months, but a rushing torrent in early spring. The flame burns year-round, although the route is less accessible when winter snows pile up in the bottom of the gorge, and the walk up the creek becomes a multi-fording adventure when snowmelt and spring rains turn the creek into a swiftly flowing, knee-deep watercourse with a slippery shale bottom. There are no bridges over the creek, although the trail markers do lead across it as many as five times before you reach the flame. The fairly rugged hike keeps all but the most motivated from frequenting the trail, helping to preserve the flame's natural setting.

The well-marked trail (the work of Eagle Scout Christian Fields) is easy to follow in summer, when you can actually walk along the nearly dry creek bed after your descent from the top of the ravine. When you reach Eternal Flame

Falls, you'll see the flame to the right; if it's not burning, just use a lighter or match to reignite it. There's not enough gas here to create a flame-up, so this is much like lighting a candle or a camp stove.

In your fascination with the naturally occurring flame, don't forget to enjoy this beautiful ravine, with its sloping walls and canopy of leafy and evergreen trees. You'll see several smaller falls cascading down the rock faces, particularly on the southwest side of the ravine, and there's a possibility of spotting small animals, frogs, and turtles along the edges of the creek.

Remember that on the way back up the trail, you will climb back to the top of the ravine, an elevation change of about 245 feet.

Miles and Directions

0.0 Begin the trail at Seufert Road. Walk into the park to a kiosk (in sight as you enter) that explains the trail markings. You will follow the blue-painted blocks of wood nailed to trees; orange diamond-shaped trail markers are also visible along most of this trail.

0.1 Here is your first creek crossing, barely a trickle in summer. Step over the creek and continue. In about 200 feet, you'll reach a wider spot in the creek. You can cross here by stepping from rock to rock, or the creek may be shallow enough to walk across.

0.2 From this point on top of the ravine, you can see the waterfall that hides the Eternal Flame. You'll begin the descent into the ravine here.

0.5 As you reach the bottom of the ravine, don't miss the blue wooden arrow that signals a sharp left turn. From here, you'll begin your walk upstream. In the next 0.2 mile, you will cross Shale Creek four times to continue to follow the blazes. In summer, you may be able to simply walk along the creek bed.

0.7 You've reached Eternal Flame Falls. Look to the right of the falls into the grotto. If you don't see the flame, you can light it easily with a lighter or match. When you are ready, turn around and retrace your steps back to the top of the ravine and Seufert Road.

1.4 You've arrived back at the trailhead at Seufert Road.

17 Erie County Forest

Here's what being "up north" is all about: thick evergreen forests growing side by side with the northeast's trademark maples and oaks—with trails for every kind of outdoor recreation.

Distance: 3.4-mile loop
Approximate hiking time: 1.5 hours
Difficulty: Moderate
Trail surface: Dirt path and dirt roads
Best season: Dec through Mar for cross-country skiing, Apr through Oct for hiking
Other trail users: Mountain bikers, horseback riders, snowmobile riders, cross-country skiers
Canine compatibility: Leashed dogs permitted
Fees and permits: None

Schedule: Open daily dawn to dusk
Maps: *National Geographic Topo! New York State* edition
Trailhead facilities: In the restrooms at the Sugar Shanty, in the parking lot on Genesee Road
Trail contact: Erie County Parks and Recreation, 95 Franklin St., Room 1359, Buffalo, NY 14202; (716) 858-8355; www.erie.gov/parks
Special considerations: Trails can be very muddy in spring and after rains. Expect to climb over fallen trees.

Finding the trailhead: Take the New York State Thruway (I-90) west to exit 54. Merge onto NY 400 South toward NY 16. Continue for 22.8 miles to the town of Holland. Turn right on Capitol Heights (this becomes Holland Glenwood Road). In 1.2 miles, turn left at Warner Gulf Road. Drive 5.3 miles to Genesee Road, and turn right. The parking lot for Erie County Forest is on the right. GPS: N42 33.100' / W78 34.328'

The Hike

Scattered throughout southern Erie County, the segments of the Erie County Forest began, for the most part, as tracts of farmland purchased from landowners in the late 1920s and 1930s. Thanks to the work of the Civilian Conservation Corps during the Great Depression, a whopping 7.5 million trees were planted on this land, creating the stands of hardwood—from black cherry to sugar maple—and evergreens (red pine, spruce, white pine, and others) that are now dense enough to block the sun and sky as you hike between them.

Managed both for wildlife preservation and commercial harvesting, the forests—particularly the two lots we explore on this hike, totaling 1,052 acres—provide the kind of wilderness experience we hope to find when we drive hundreds of miles into the mountains or toward the American West. Snow-coated conifers emphasize the sense of being "in the North Country" in winter, while the abundance of nesting bird species in spring and summer underscore the value this young forest has for restoring wildlife habitat. Squirrels and chipmunks rule the forest, but it's not uncommon to spot tiny gray shrews nosing through the understory, or beavers in the pond area. Deer sightings are a near certainty in early morning and at dusk.

The combination of the Silent Woods Trail in the forest's north section with the Old Scarbuck Trail to the south creates a significant loop, with a gradual elevation change of nearly 220 feet. You'll walk trails with hardwoods on one side and evergreens on the other, pass through thickly wooded areas, and climb over or circumnavigate fallen limbs and trunks that block the trail—all while enjoying the fragrances and colors of the woods, even as winter's monochromatic shades settle over the forest.

Miles and Directions

0.0   Begin the trail at the parking lot with the Sugar Shanty on Genesee Road. Head north through the lot to the gravel road that leads up the hill. This is one of the steepest short climbs you'll make on this hike, so let's get it done first.

0.2   The blue trail heads off to the left, through the forest. Continue up the hill. You will see bits of yellow ribbon tied to the new trees on your right, and horse trail markers on trees to your left. Continue up the hill.

0.5   At the top of the hill, you'll see the Sugarbush Shack. Turn right on the gravel road.

0.6   Cross a little stream here. In about 250 feet, the trail goes straight and to the right. Continue straight until you see the orange blazes ahead. This is the statewide blaze color for the Conservation Trail, run by the Finger Lakes Trail Conference. We'll follow part of that trail through the forest.

0.7   When you get to the orange-blazed trail, turn right and start through the woods. Notice that the trail is also blazed yellow—that's the Silent Woods Trail. Continue to follow yellow and orange.

1.0   Turn left as the trail enters an area with fewer trees.

1.1   Cross the "Bridge on the River Kwai" over Dresser Creek. Bear right after the bridge.

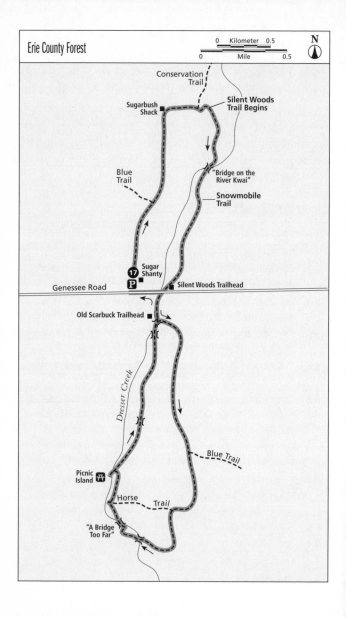

1.2 At the unmarked intersection with the dirt road, turn right on the road and watch for the yellow blazes on your left. Follow the blazes into the woods.

1.4 You've emerged from the woods on Genesee Road, at the official trailhead for the Silent Woods Trail. If you've had enough hiking, the parking lot is just down the road to your right. If you're going to continue down the Old Scarbuck Trail, cross the road and stop at the Finger Lakes Trail shack for information, and to look at a larger map of the trails in this part of the forest. Then follow the yellow blazes into the woods.

1.9 At the intersection with the blue trail here, go right and continue on the yellow trail.

2.1 Cross the intersection and bear right on the yellow trail.

2.2 Turn left and follow the yellow and orange blazes. The horse trail goes straight here.

2.3 There's a little bridge here, then a short, steep descent to a bridge over the creek. Once you've crossed, stop to enjoy the particularly nice view of the creek winding through the woods.

2.4 Here you have a choice: The yellow trail goes in two directions, straight and to the left. If you'd like a longer hike, cross "A Bridge Too Far" over the creek here and continue around the Southern Loop (which will bring you back to this point in about 0.5 mile). If you'd rather start back, go straight up the Old Scarbuck Trail by following the yellow blazes straight ahead.

2.6 The yellow trail and the horse trail intersect here. The horse trail goes into the creek. Turn right to continue on the yellow trail's return route.

2.7 If you like, make a stop here at Picnic Island. Sturdy bridges cross the creek to take you to a seating area with picnic tables, a stone grill, benches, and a (nonworking) stone well. When you're ready, continue on the yellow trail going north.

2.9 Cross the partial bridge over the creek.

3.1 Here's another small bridge over the creek.

3.2 Here is the bridge you crossed earlier on your way into this part of the woods. You've reached Genesee Road. It's a short walk from here back to the parking lot and your car.

3.4 You've reached the parking lot.

18 Deer Lick Conservation Area

Meadows, mature forests, a former orchard, and falling waters tumbling into the 400-foot-deep canyon—these treats and more await you in this National Natural Landmark.

Distance: 3.5 miles out-and-back

Approximate hiking time: 1.5 hours

Difficulty: Moderate

Trail surface: Dirt path

Best season: Apr through Oct

Other trail users: Snowshoers and cross-country skiers

Canine compatibility: No pets permitted

Fees and permits: None

Schedule: Open daily dawn to dusk

Maps: Available from The Nature Conservancy, www.nature.org

Trailhead facilities: None; water at Melissa's Spring has not been tested.

Trail contact: The Nature Conservancy, Western New York Project Office, 10 Main St., Cattaraugus, NY 14719; (716) 257-3689; www.nature.org

Special considerations: Trails can be very muddy in spring and after rains.

Finding the trailhead: From Buffalo, take US 62 to Gowanda. Turn on South Water Street, which becomes Commercial Street, and then Palmer Street. Turn right on Broadway Road, and continue for about 1 mile to Point Peter Road. Turn left on Point Peter and watch for the parking lot, at the top of the second hill past Forty Road. GPS: N42 25.203' / W78 54.318'

The Hike

The South Branch of Cattaraugus Creek played an instrumental role in shaping Deer Lick Conservation Area, a natural treasure protected by The Nature Conservancy. Preserved since the 1960s through the foresight of three generous landowners, Deer Lick remains an unaffected collection of ancient forests, open meadows, creeks, waterfalls, and a splendid canyon.

The most impressive feature of this remarkable preserve, the 400-foot-deep canyon, carved by the creek, becomes visible through the dense hardwoods as you walk along the canyon's ridgeline.

Here ancient old-growth forests of sugar maple, hemlock, black cherry, and American beech have thrived for hundreds of years, growing to 100 feet and higher. Trained eyes can spot young American chestnut trees in the mix, part of a project to return this species to its natural habitat and eradicate the Asian blight that virtually wiped out the chestnuts in the early twentieth century.

This is one of the few places in western New York where it's possible (though rare) to spot a black bear, and bald eagles have been known to soar over the canyon or perch at the tops of the tallest trees. All of the area's common woodland creatures live here, from gray squirrel to raccoon, and the creek provides a hospitable environment for rare aquatic species, including the eastern sand darter and tiger beetles. Steelhead trout also thrive in these waters.

This hike follows the ridgeline above the canyon, providing expansive views of the walls across the creek and of Ensminger Falls (which flow only in the spring) on the other side of the wide canyon. Additional easy trails—including

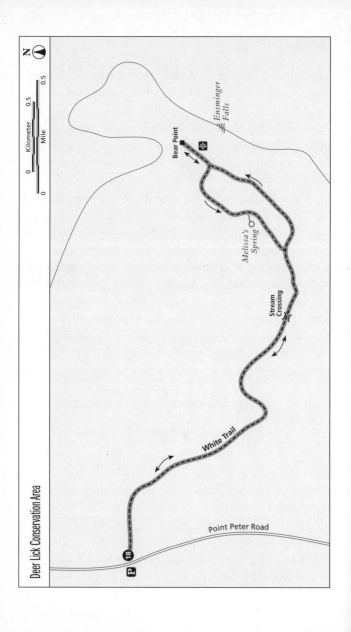

the routes blazed red and orange—take you through open meadow and along Deer Lick Creek, while the yellow trail allows you to descend into Deer Lick Ravine for a view from the top of Deer Lick Falls.

On the return leg of the white trail, you'll come upon Melissa's Spring, a natural seep that bubbles to the surface at the bottom of a slight hill. The spring's clear water has been brought within reach by a pipe on a simple stand. The Nature Conservancy has never tested this water for potability, so drinking is not recommended.

A word to the wise: Private landowners with property adjacent to this preserve have no patience with trespassers. Be sure to obey all signs warning hikers off of posted lands. There's plenty of preserved land to explore here without inviting trouble on private property. You may wish to check with The Nature Conservancy website at www .nature.org before hiking here, to be sure that the protected lands are still open to visitors.

Miles and Directions

0.0 Begin the trail at the parking lot. All trails begin from the same point.

0.2 The trails diverge here: red, yellow, orange, and white. Follow the white trail (take the right fork).

0.5 The red trail goes left. It's a loop trail that will come out shortly. If you like, you can lengthen your hike by adding this loop.

0.6 The orange trail goes right here. This loop crosses hilly terrain along Deer Lick Creek. You can extend your hike by taking this loop, which will bring you back to the white trail a few feet from here.

0.7 The yellow trail goes left here. This is a more difficult trail, which leads to a view of Deer Lick Falls from the top. You can extend your hike by taking this trail as well. If you're continuing on the white trail, go straight.

0.9 Cross a stream here by stepping on the rocks. This is a little trickier in spring, but is still pretty easy to navigate.

1.1 The white and yellow trails diverge here again. Stay on the white trail, to the right. Here you begin a fairly steady ascent to a terrific view of the gorge. Watch to your right as you hike for glimpses of the gorge walls and the creek, some 400 feet below.

1.5 Look to the right here for a great view of Ensminger Falls, a 140-foot cascade that flows only in spring and summer. It's an especially exciting sight in Mar and Apr. Continue another 350 feet to the end of Bear Point, where you can enjoy a view of the gorge—though it's partially occluded by the thick forestation here. When you're ready, begin to head back down the point.

1.6 Bear right here for a different route back.

1.8 The yellow and white trails meet here. Continue straight on the white trail.

1.9 Here is Melissa's Spring. You'll see a pipe balanced on a metal frame with a trickle of water emerging from it. This water flows from a natural spring underground. As the water has not been tested for potability, drinking is not recommended. From here, continue straight on the white trail.

2.0 From here, you'll return on the same route you followed to come into the preserve. If you like, try one of the side loops (red or orange) before you return to your vehicle.

3.5 You've reached the parking lot.

19 Beaver Meadow Audubon Center

This delightful preserve trail wanders through hardwood and spruce forests, past glacially sculpted kettle ponds, and across an open field and arboretum.

Distance: 2.1-mile loop
Approximate hiking time: 1 hour
Difficulty: Easy
Trail surface: Dirt path with some boardwalk
Best season: Apr through June; Sept through Nov
Other trail users: Cross-country skiers and snowshoeing hikers in winter
Canine compatibility: No pets allowed

Fees and permits: Small donation requested
Schedule: Open daily dawn to dusk
Maps: Buffalo Audubon Society, www.buffaloaudubon.com/centers.htm
Trailhead facilities: At visitor center
Trail contact: Buffalo Audubon Society, 1610 Welch Rd., North Java, NY 14113; (585) 457-3228; www.buffaloaudubon.com

Finding the trailhead: From the city of Buffalo, take I-190 East to I-90 West (toward Erie). Take exit 54 for NY 400. Merge onto NY 400 South and continue to the US 20A / NY 78 exit toward East Aurora. Follow US 20A / NY 78 about 11 miles to Cattaraugus Road (NY 77); turn right. Continue 6.8 miles on Cattaraugus Road to Welch Road. Turn left at Welch Road. The nature center will appear on your right, at 1610 Welch Rd. in North Java. GPS N42 40.396' / W78 23.078'

The Hike

Tucked away in rural Wyoming County, Beaver Meadow Audubon Center protects a remarkable selection of healthy habitats, making its forests, meadows, marshland, and ponds accessible to thousands of visitors every year—especially children, who come with their classmates, Scout troops, and fellow campers to hike in the wilderness and make a connection with the natural world. It's not surprising, then, that the preserve's navigation includes more than two dozen named, labeled trails—some of them barely 0.25 mile long—to lead visitors to a striking variety of natural features, wildlife-viewing opportunities, and peaceful retreats in the more remote corners of the preserve.

For the first-time visitor, the wealth of trail options can be dizzying. We recommend the variety offered by Long Trail, a perimeter hike through maple, oak, moosewood, sassafras, elm, birch, and other hardwood species, moving gradually into a predominantly spruce forest intermingled with pine and other evergreens. Pileated woodpeckers frequent these woods, and songbirds make this area a migratory stopover in spring and fall. White-tailed deer tracks are everywhere along the trail, and the tiny footprints of mink, mice, voles, and other small woodland creatures are easy to see just after a rain or in the winter snow.

Beyond the woods, your hike will take you through low marshland and past blue kettle ponds, created by glaciers that left big blocks of ice, or *calves,* in their wake as they receded at the end of the last ice age. When the ice blocks melted, they filled the holes left behind with water and sediment, forming these small, deep ponds that provide an important water source for amphibians, fish, and water-loving mammals. Beaver Pond no longer supports a beaver family, but the lodge built by the last residents still stands in the middle of the pond; it's easy to see from the visitor center's wide windows, or as you approach the visitor center at the end of your hike.

Finally, plan to spend some time in the Arboretum, an open area in which Buffalo Audubon has planted some carefully chosen trees to observe their growth. There's a detailed display that will help you identify the species you see here and others throughout the preserve.

Miles and Directions

0.0 Park in the parking lot near the visitor center, and cross Welch Road to the Kettle Pond Trail sign. In about 200 feet the Cucumber Hill Trail begins; continue straight on the Kettle Pond Trail. Pass the Grouse Nest trailhead.

0.1 Turn right slightly at the KETTLE POND TRAIL sign, and then leave the pond and head straight through the woods on the Nuthatch Trail (which is unmarked). Walk up the incline for about 250 feet and turn right onto Mitchell Trail. Cucumber Hill Trail goes to the left; continue on Mitchell. In another 100 feet, turn left onto Long Trail. You'll follow the orange blazes from here, as well as the yellow-and-green metal arrow signs attached to the trees under the blazes.

0.2 Hawk Ridge Trail goes left here. Continue straight, past Field Sparrow Trail on your right.

0.6 Tanglewood Trail, a short lollipop trail, goes to your left. This is a nice 0.25-mile addition if you care to add it to your hike. In about 150 feet down Long Trail, Hidden Valley Trail goes to the right. Take Long Trail, which goes left here.

0.7 Puddle Pond Trail goes right. Continue straight on Long Trail.

0.8 A boardwalk crosses a marshy area here.

0.9 Rusty Stove Trail goes right. Continue to follow Long Trail, straight ahead.

1.0 A small loop trail called the Backwoods Trail goes left here. Long Trail goes right; continue to follow that. (*Note:* Backwoods Loop also has orange blazes.)

1.1 A bridge here crosses a small stream.

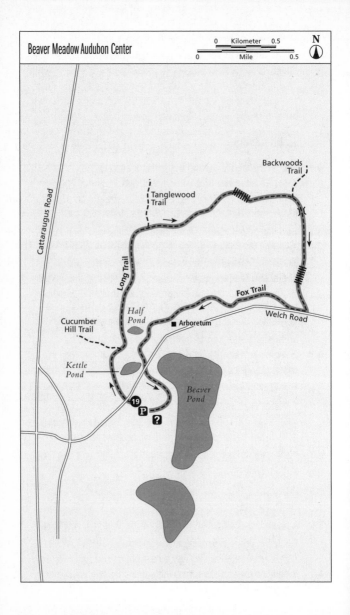

Beaver Meadow Audubon Center

0   Kilometer   0.5

0   Mile   0.5

N

Cattaraugus Road

Backwoods
Trail

Tanglewood
Trail

Long Trail

Fox Trail

Welch Road

Cucumber
Hill Trail

Half
Pond

Arboretum

Kettle
Pond

Beaver
Pond

19

P

?

1.3 Cross another boardwalk over the marsh.

1.4 Go up a steep, short incline and emerge on Welch Road. Long Trail ends here. Turn right on the road and walk to Fox Trail, reentering the woods on the right about 300 feet from the end of Long Trail. You'll see a difference in the habitat here—a shift from hardwood and spruce forest to lower shrubs and a more open landscape. In about 250 feet, Old Bones Trail goes right. Continue straight on Fox Trail.

1.7 You've arrived at an open meadow, with a scattering of cultivated trees. Hawk Watch Trail goes right. Cross the field to your left on the mowed path to continue to Fox Trail. You're approaching the Arboretum. Continue straight past the Puddle Pond Trail, which emerges on your right.

1.8 You're in the Arboretum. Fencing surrounds many of the young trees in this area, a precaution that keeps animals from nibbling on their young shoots. Hidden Valley Trail goes to the right here, and there's an education shelter on the left with information about the trees and the many varieties of vegetation that thrive throughout the nature center. Continue straight ahead on Field Sparrow Trail.

1.9 Bear left on Possum Crossing Trail. In a few steps, you'll reach Half Pond, a pleasant place for a rest (there's a bench overlooking the pond). Wood duck boxes provide safe nesting for these beautiful birds in early spring. When you're ready, proceed down Possum Crossing Trail; cross Mitchell Trail and continue straight.

2.0 You've come to Kettle Pond. Turn left and follow the pond trail around until you reach Welch Road. Cross the road and turn right; you'll reach Beaver Pond Trail in a few steps. Turn left from the road onto this trail.

2.1 The Beaver Meadow Visitor Center is on your right. Stop here for water, restrooms, and excellent displays about local wildlife, plants, and trees, and record your bird and animal sightings in the logbook. There's a nice gift shop here as well. When you're ready, return to the parking lot and your vehicle.

20 Zoar Valley Multiple Use Area: Valentine Flats Trail

Follow a ridgeline along a ravine wall, stroll through a hardwood forest, and arrive at the confluence of two wide, burbling creeks in this ruggedly beautiful place.

Distance: 2.2 miles out-and-back
Approximate hiking time: 1 hour
Difficulty: Moderate
Trail surface: Dirt path
Best season: Apr through Oct
Other trail users: Anglers, paddlers, and others on the way to the creek
Canine compatibility: Leashed dogs permitted
Fees and permits: None
Schedule: Open daily dawn to dusk
Maps: NYS Department of Environmental Conservation, www

.dec.ny.gov/docs/lands_ forests_pdf/zoarfig5.pdf
Trailhead facilities: None (creek water requires purification)
Trail contact: Zoar Valley Nature Society, P.O. Box 55, Gowanda, NY 14070; (716) 380-1430; www.zoarvalley.org
Special considerations: Avoid trail edges, as underlying shale may have fallen away, creating an unstable ledge. Do not trespass on posted lands around Zoar Valley Multiple Use Area, as an arrest may result.

Finding the trailhead: From Buffalo, take US 62 to Gowanda. Turn left on Buffalo Street, which will curve into East Main Street in 0.6 mile. Cross the bridge and turn left at the next light onto South Water Street. Turn right at Broadway, and continue 0.9 mile to Point Peter Road. Turn left and follow Point Peter about a mile to Valentine Flats Road; turn left. The road dead-ends at the trailhead parking lot. GPS: N42 26.652' / W78 54.165'

The Hike

For sheer scenic majesty, Zoar Valley offers one of the finest experiences in western New York, combining old-growth forests, the powerful flow of two major waterways, and an erosion-sculpted ravine still influenced by gravity, wind, and weather. Adventurers come here to run the Class III rapids, anglers find excellent fishing, and hikers can't resist edging along the sides of the ravine to some of the area's most enticing views.

Cliffs rise to 400 feet above the main and south branches of Cattaraugus Creek, the wide canyon floor becoming a floodplain in rainy seasons. The surrounding soil nurtures some of the area's tallest and most impressive trees, exceeding 150 feet in height with histories that extend for centuries. Indeed, hikers find a sense of the ancient here, and a relief that this virtually untouched wilderness remains undisturbed by development. Surrounding landowners jealously guard this land in full appreciation of its significance as a natural resource. Because of this guardianship, only a few areas of this preserve are open to public exploration, helping to keep this unusual place safe from harm.

The Valentine Flats Trail takes hikers on a direct route to the conjunction of Cattaraugus Creek's main and south branches, at the base of the canyon and the edge of a section of mature hardwood forest. This is one of the best places in the area to enjoy Zoar's most beautiful features—especially in late fall, when the trees turn scarlet, amber, and tangerine, filling the valley with layer upon layer of their brilliant shades.

A word about those adjacent landowners: Other authors' books have suggested that private lands surrounding the

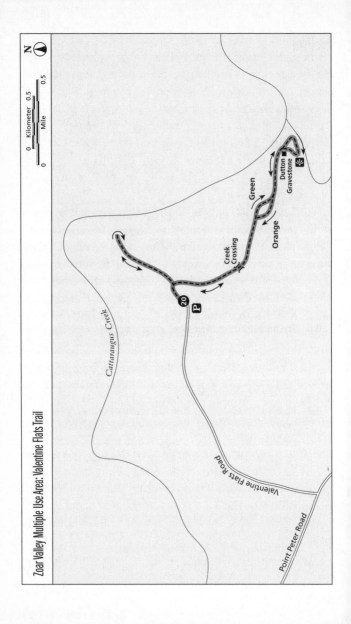

Zoar Valley Multiple Use Area: Valentine Flats Trail

Cattaraugus Creek

Creek Crossing

Green

Orange

Dutton Gravestone

Valentine Flats Road

Point Peter Road

N

0   Kilometer   0.5

0   Mile   0.5

multiple use area are open to the public. They are not, and are posted accordingly. Please respect these postings and do not trespass; the issue has become so pronounced that trespassers are now arrested and charged. Be safe, not sorry, and enjoy the valley from the trails.

Miles and Directions

0.0 Begin the trail at the parking lot. After a few feet the trail forks. Take the right fork (you'll come back and explore to the left later). Follow the orange and green blazes, which go in the same direction. You'll walk along a ridge on the ravine; the trail is narrow in some places, with drop-offs of 100 feet or more. Watch your step.

0.3 A stream comes down from the top of the gorge and crosses the trail here, with no bridge. Step across on stones (it's shallow even in the spring). Continue on the orange- and green-blazed trail.

0.5 The orange and green trails diverge here. Take the green trail (left), on the clearer path. You'll take the other trail on the way back.

0.6 The green and orange paths converge again here. Continue to the left on the orange path.

0.8 Here you have your first view of Cattaraugus Creek, down the ravine to your right. About 250 feet ahead on the path, there's a headstone for Thomas Dutton. Dutton, a resident of nearby Lodi, met an untimely end in the valley during the fall of 1826, when he drowned in the creek. By the time his body was discovered the following spring, it was too decomposed to determine if he'd died through accident or criminal mischief. The $400 and silver watch he'd been carrying were long gone, however, so thievery continues as the consensus. His remains are buried beneath this stone.

0.9 You've come to one of two dramatic viewpoints of the joining of the two creek branches and the surrounding ravine.

Continue around the bend in the creek about 250 feet to the best vantage point, from which you can enjoy an expansive vista of the creeks, rock walls, trees grasping for footing against the ravine edge, and the surrounding floodplain. When you're ready, turn around and retrace your steps to the spot where the orange and green trails diverged.

1.2 This time, take the orange trail (to the left). You'll cross a small creek on rocks, and walk a less-worn path closer to the ravine wall. Rejoin the combined orange and green trails, and continue back to the first fork in the trail, near the parking lot.

1.7 Instead of turning left here and proceeding to your car, continue straight ahead.

1.9 The short trail (with a steep drop-off on the right side) leads to a stunning overlook, from which you can view the ravine and the creek some 400 feet below. Keep back from the edge here, as shale falling from underneath has turned this into a fairly precarious ledge. When you're ready, turn back and return to the parking area.

2.1 Turn right at the fork. This is the path to the parking lot.

2.2 You've reached your vehicle.

Clubs and Trail Groups

- Adirondack Mountain Club, Niagara Frontier Chapter, www.adk-nfc.org. The club offers a variety of hikes and programs to share the joy and knowledge of outdoor recreation.

- Buffalo Audubon Society, 1610 Welch Rd., North Java, NY 14113; (800) 377-1520; www.buffaloaudubon.com. With several preserves of its own, Buffalo Audubon promotes appreciation and enjoyment of the natural world. Look for events and hikes on its Web site.

- Buffalo Niagara Riverkeeper, 617 Main St., Suite M108, Buffalo, NY 14203; (716) 852-7483; www.bnriverkeeper.org. This organization improves public waterfront access, restores watershed ecology, and conserves the river heritage.

- Buffalo Outdoors Meetup Group, hiking.meetup.com/cities/us/ny/buffalo. Hiking, bicycling, rock climbing, and ice skating are some of the many activities this social group schedules.

- Chautauqua Rails to Trails, Route 394 in the Train Depot, P.O. Box 151, Mayville, NY 14757; (716) 269-3666; www.chaurtt.org. This organization is dedicated to the preservation of abandoned rail corridors as trails for recreational use.

- Foothills Trail Club, www.foothillstrailclub.org. Creators of the 177-mile Conservation Trail, this group's membership is dedicated to building and maintaining trails, aiding in the conservation of wild lands and wildlife, and promoting good fellowship through hikes and nature.

- Western New York Land Conservancy, 21 South Grove St., Room 120, East Aurora, NY 14052; (716) 687-1225; www.wnylc.org. This nonprofit land trust works to preserve open space and farmland in eight counties of western New York State.

About the Author

Randi Minetor has written eighteen books to date for Globe Pequot Press (GPP), including the first three *Passport to Your National Parks® Companion Guides,* and *National Park Pocket Guides* for Great Smoky Mountains, Zion and Bryce Canyon, Acadia, and Everglades National Parks. She has also written a *Pocket Guide for Gulf Islands National Seashore* and five books in the Timeline Tours series. Her husband, Nic Minetor, is the photographer for her Pocket Guides and Timeline Tours books. Randi is also the National Parks Recreation Examiner on Examiner.com. She and Nic live in Rochester.